JESUS AND THE KINGDOM OF GOD

BY

HAROLD ROBERTS, M.A., Ph.D.
*Professor of Systematic Theology and Philosophy of Religion,
Richmond College*

WIPF & STOCK · Eugene, Oregon

Wipf and Stock Publishers
199 W 8th Ave, Suite 3
Eugene, OR 97401

Jesus and the Kingdom of God
By Roberts, Harold
Copyright©1955 Epworth Press
ISBN 13: 978-1-60608-725-1
Publication date 5/7/2009
Previously published by Epworth Press, 1955

Copyright © Epworth Press 1955
First English edition1955 by Epworth Press
This edition published by arrangement with Epworth Press

PREFACE

THE AIM of the following pages is to consider the theological implications of the teaching of Jesus in the Synoptic Gospels about the Kingdom of God. During recent years, significant contributions have been made by biblical scholars to the study of the idea of the Kingdom of God, and the time has come to inquire how far it can be claimed that the results throw light on the central doctrines of the Christian Faith. In spite of wide divergencies of interpretation, there is a growing recognition that the Christian message is set in an eschatological framework. That is, it is governed by the conception of the ultimate purpose of God for man and the universe—the End to which all history under the judgement of divine grace is moving. At one time, a book on systematic theology dealt with eschatology when every other doctrine had been expounded. It seemed entirely fitting that the 'last things' should be reserved for the final chapter. Today, it is being urged that every doctrine should be related to eschatology. There are those who speak of the dawn of a new theological epoch and a new terminology is certainly being evolved which, by comparison, makes the language of traditional theology pale into complete intelligibility. Without indulging in extravagant claims, it may be said that the rediscovery of biblical eschatology suggests a theological approach which may leave a permanent mark on the life and thought of the Church.

No attempt will be made in this work to deal in any detail with controversial points of exegesis or to cover ground that has been well ploughed by learned and 'popular' treatments of the concept of the Kingdom of God during the past two decades. What seems to be more important is that we should try to discover whether linguistic and exegetical studies of the eschatology of the Gospels provide us with a new and deeper understanding of the foundations of the Christian Faith which can be preached and set forth in such a way that all who have a religious interest will be able to grasp its significance.

I have to thank Professor F. Bertram Clogg, M.A., B.D., Principal of Richmond College, Surrey, for reading the proofs and for many acts of kindness in the course of a happy colleagueship.

It is also a pleasant duty to acknowledge my gratitude to the Trustees for honouring me with an invitation to deliver the Fernley-Hartley Lecture 1954. Finally, I would express my deep appreciation of the patience and courtesy of the Rev. Frank H. Cumbers, B.A., B.D., of the Epworth Press in view of the delay in the delivery of the manuscript.

HAROLD ROBERTS

RICHMOND COLLEGE
SURREY 1954

CONTENTS

PREFACE 5

INTRODUCTION 9

1. THE KINGDOM OF GOD IN THE TEACHING OF JESUS . 21

2. THE DOCTRINE OF GOD 43

3. THE PERSON OF CHRIST 67

4. THE CHURCH 84

5. THE CHRISTIAN HOPE 102

INDEX OF NAMES 121

INDEX OF SCRIPTURE REFERENCES 123

INTRODUCTION

DURING the past thirty years, changes have taken place in theological thought which may have an important bearing on the life and worship of the Christian Church. There has been a movement away from the theological liberalism of the nineteenth and early twentieth century and while much of the criticism directed against liberalism shows a lamentable lack of appreciation of its undoubted achievements, it must be admitted that its treatment of the New Testament sometimes obscured the Christ of faith and that its message failed to meet man at the point of his deepest need. Recent developments have been conditioned partly by a rediscovery of the unity of the Bible, and partly by the succession of world-crises which culminated in the moral and spiritual disaster of two world wars. The key to what may be justly described as a theological revival is to be found in the attempt to reinterpret the meaning and implications of the central theme of the Old and New Testament: the Kingdom of God. In order that we may gain an understanding of the nature and significance of the present debate, it will be an advantage to trace briefly some of its antecedents although many names which would appear in a complete survey of the relevant literature must regrettably be omitted.

The theological renascence of today is a reaction not so much from the interpretation of the Kingdom of God in the writings of Johannes Weiss and Schweitzer as from the theology of Ritschl and his followers who propounded a view of the Kingdom of God for which contemporary New Testament scholarship can find no warrant. By the Kingdom of God Ritschl and his school largely meant the moral unification of humanity through action prompted by universal love.[1] Ritschl sought to hold together the doctrine of redemption through Christ and the conception of the Kingdom of God as the ethical ideal for every Christian. Hence, to use his well-known simile, Christianity is to be compared, not to a circle described from one centre, but to an ellipse which is determined by two foci.[2] His emphasis, however, on what he understood

[1] Ritschl, *The Christian Doctrine of Justification and Reconciliation* (E.T., H. R. Mackintosh and A. B. Macaulay), p. 280.
[2] ibid., p. 11.

by the Kingdom led to the subordination of personal redemption through Christ to the organization of humanity on the basis of love, and unintentionally he made religion the handmaid of morality.

His view that, 'in every religion, what is sought, with the help of the superhuman spiritual power reverenced by man, is a solution of the contradiction in which man finds himself as both a part of nature and a spiritual personality claiming to dominate nature'[3] is in obvious harmony with the conception of God as the guarantor and agent of the ideal community which is the goal of human endeavour.

A similar interpretation is found among the followers of Ritschl. Kaftan in his earlier works, *The Truth of the Christian Religion* and *The Essence of the Christian Religion*, speaks of the Kingdom as the chief good of humanity and as our supreme ideal, and Hermann in his book on *Religion in Relation to our Knowledge of the World and Morality* describes it as the universal moral community. In spite of the emphasis in Hermann's better-known volume, *The Communion of the Christian with God*, on an individual piety that is grounded in the historical Jesus as the revelation of God to each believer, the idea of the Kingdom as a moral commonwealth is regulative for his theology. The influence of Ritschlianism was widespread in the nineteenth and early twentieth centuries, and there is no doubt that it has left its mark upon the thought of the Church. An examination of the phraseology and content of modern preaching and liturgies reveals a doctrine of the Kingdom which has more in common with the teaching of Ritschl than with that of the New Testament. The conception of the Kingdom as a moral commonwealth which is organized on the basis of love makes a strong appeal to an age which is acutely conscious of social injustice and rightly impatient of the kind of piety that becomes a way of escape from social responsibilities.

In this country, a similar view of the Kingdom of God was advanced during the nineteenth century. Seeley's *Ecce Homo* can hardly claim to be a work of New Testament scholarship, but it will long be cherished as one of the more valuable treasures of religious literature and it has moulded the thinking of many who are largely unacquainted with the labours of biblical scholars. Throughout this book, published in 1886, the Kingdom is

[3] ibid., p. 199.

represented as a theocracy, and in the fourth chapter on Christ's Royalty we read: 'Christ, in describing himself as a king, and at the same time as king of the Kingdom of God—in other words as a king representing the Majesty of the Invisible King of a theocracy —claimed the character first of Founder, next of Legislator, thirdly, in a certain high and peculiar sense, of Judge, of a new divine society.'[4] Again the kingdom as a community is set forth in a volume published by Professor A. B. Bruce in 1889 which had a remarkable sale—at least, for a theological work. Its title is *The Kingdom of God*. He contends that salvation consists in citizenship in the divine commonwealth, and for him the Kingdom of God as thus conceived is an exhaustive category for theology. It should be added that Professor Bruce recognizes the presence of the Apocalyptic element in the teaching of Jesus, although he does not regard it as in any sense fundamental.

While this clear-cut and seemingly intelligible conception of the Kingdom as a divine society dependent for its realization upon the ethical obedience of its members was being confidently proclaimed, attention was being directed elsewhere to those passages in the Gospels which appeared to teach that the existing order was about to crumble amid scenes of unprecedented desolation and that with its dissolution the Kingdom of God would be ushered in by the Son of Man. The wicked would receive the punishment which they deserved and the elect would sit down with Abraham, Isaac and Jacob in the heavenly Kingdom. Renan, in his romantic *Life of Jesus*, while admitting that apocalyptic and spiritual elements are intertwined in the teaching of Jesus about the Kingdom, exposes what he believes to be the false hopes about the imminent end of all things which Jesus and his followers entertained. At about the same time, Strauss followed up his earlier 'Life of Jesus', first published in 1835, in which he had dealt with the prophecies of Jesus about the end of the age, with a particularly virulent attack on the utterances of Jesus about the future Kingdom and His own place within it. The new work was entitled *The Life of Jesus for the German People*. He was indeed less incensed by the erroneous philosophy of history which the predictions of Jesus involved than by the fanatical claims which He made for Himself as judge of His fellows.

[4] The New Universal Library edition (Routledge), p. 33.

The battle was now joined, and in spite of the blatant dogmatism of Strauss' writings, the presence of the apocalyptic passages in the Gospels could no longer be ignored. These passages divided scholars into opposing schools. There were some who regarded the apocalyptic element as incidental, others who thought it all-important, and yet others who took the view that it was imported into the Gospels and formed no part of the authentic tradition of the words of Jesus.

In the year 1892 Johannes Weiss published a little book entitled *The Preaching of Jesus on the Kingdom of God*. He repudiated the interpretation of the Kingdom advanced by Schleiermacher, Ritschl, and Kaftan, and put in its place the view that Jesus believed that the Kingdom belonged to the near future, that it was to come by a supernatural catastrophic act, and that at its coming He would be made both Lord and Messiah. The old order was to be destroyed at the Parousia, or the return of Christ upon the clouds of heaven, which would be accompanied by universal judgement and the setting-up of the new Kingdom where all nations would serve God in righteousness and truth. Jesus, we are told, at one time believed that the Kingdom would be established in His life-time, but He came to see that it could be brought in only by His treading the path of death. Palestine was to become the centre of the new Kingdom, and in the new Israel which was to absorb the Gentiles Jesus and His faithful followers would rule. God alone could bring in the Kingdom and His kingly reign would be fulfilled in the reign of the Messiah. The ethical teaching of Jesus was a provisional or 'interim' ethic, intended to serve the needs of the disciples in the critical days that remained before the End came. Weiss examined the texts and parables which have figured so prominently in recent investigations and although in a later edition (1900), which was virtually a new book, he left room for elements in the teaching of Jesus which were not covered by the extreme eschatology which he advocated in the earlier work, his fundamental position seemed to be unchanged.[5]

Harnack's *What is Christianity?* (1900) represents a very different approach. He recognizes that Jesus was profoundly conscious of the conflict between the Kingdom of God and the kingdom of

---

[5] *The Idea of the Kingdom of God in Theology* (1901) is a most valuable contribution to historical theology.

evil which can only be resolved by a decisive battle. He saw the Kingdom of God triumphant and Himself seated at the right hand of the Father, with the disciples on thrones judging the twelve tribes of Israel. But for Harnack it is not in these dramatic pictures that we see unveiled the peculiar significance of the teaching of Jesus about the Kingdom. The idea of the two kingdoms He shared with His contemporaries. What was specially characteristic of His teaching was His emphasis on the Kingdom as something supernatural, a purely religious blessing, the inner link with the living God, a power that works inwardly, bringing healing and above all the forgiveness of sins. 'Eternal life came in and made the world look new.'[6] Though Harnack's interpretation of the Gospel omits much that is fundamental, to dismiss it as a species of social idealism, and nothing more, is an inexcusable caricature of his conception of the Kingdom of God as the eternal entering into time.

It was in 1901 that there appeared a small book by Albert Schweitzer, a young assistant minister at Strassburg, entitled *The Lord's Supper*. In the second part of this work, published in an English translation in 1925 under the title *The Mystery of the Kingdom of God*, we have a sketch of the life of Jesus which, in spite of its revolutionary character, created nothing in the nature of a sensation in Germany. The book by which he is best known in this country and which introduced English students to his views is *The Quest of the Historical Jesus*, first published in Germany in 1906 and followed by a second edition in 1913. The English translation appeared in 1910,[7] and it soon became obvious that, in spite of the violent reaction to a view of Jesus and His teaching which many regarded as blasphemous, the place of eschatology[8] in the Gospels could no longer be regarded as an optional subject by New Testament scholars and theologians. A fresh impetus was given, not only to the study of the New Testament evidence, but to the examination of the Apocalyptic

---

[6] *What is Christianity?* (E.T.), p. 62.

[7] For the third edition (1954) Schweitzer has written a new introduction in which he reaffirms his original position.

[8] In manuals of theology, 'eschatology' has generally been taken to refer to the study of 'the last things'—death, judgement, heaven, hell. Here we shall apply the term to the study of the ultimate transcendent end to which all history moves in the providence of God. Apocalyptic is the name given to the type of literature which belongs roughly to the last two centuries B.C. and the first century A.D. It contains revelations of the End through visions, allegories, and symbolism.

literature, which was being investigated, in the light of new material by the late R. H. Charles and his colleagues. What was it in the contentions of Schweitzer that created such stir, particularly in the relatively peaceful realm of English theology? The greater part of his famous book is concerned to undermine the foundations of the various attempts which had been made to write a 'Liberal' life of Jesus from Reimarus to Wrede. He complains that most of his predecessors have ignored the teaching of Jesus about the Kingdom as an imminent and catastrophic event, and in the last two chapters supplies a 'constructive' sketch which, in spite of its occasional flashes of insight, reveals the critical defects so strongly condemned by the author in his review of previous works. According to Schweitzer, the mind of Jesus was dominated by the belief in the imminent coming of the Kingdom, which would be preceded in rapid succession by the Messianic woes or tribulations, the appearance of the Son of Man on the clouds, the resurrection of the dead, and the Last Judgement. Jesus, it would seem, expected that the Son of Man would come in glory before the disciples whom He sent out had completed their preaching-tour in the cities of Israel (Mt 10^{23}). But the disciples returned, and neither the final woes nor the Kingdom had arrived. It was therefore necessary for Him to reconsider His course of action. He comes to the conclusion that the Messianic woes must be endured by Himself alone, and that they would be borne by Him in order that the people might go free. He must give His life a ransom for many (Mk 10^{45}). Hence, He deliberately went to Jerusalem believing that by His death He would cause Israel to repent and thus force the coming of the Kingdom. He was impelled by the conviction, not that He was the Messiah or the Son of Man, but that in the coming Kingdom He would be the Messiah. This conviction was revealed at Caesarea Philippi, but it was kept as a secret from those without the inner circle, and all but his closest followers were allowed to think of Him as the coming Elijah, the herald, according to later Judaism, of the Messiah. His claim to be the Messiah of the Kingdom was betrayed by Judas to the chief priests and acknowledged by Jesus Himself before Caiaphas. The journey to Jerusalem was thus 'the funeral march to victory'. Jesus, in the memorable words so often quoted, 'lays hold of the wheel of the world to set it moving on that last revolution which is to bring all

INTRODUCTION 15

ordinary history to a close. It refuses to turn and He throws Himself upon it. Then it does turn and crushes Him. Instead of bringing in the eschatological conditions, He has destroyed them. The wheel rolls onward, and the mangled body of the one immeasurably great Man, who was strong enough to think of Himself as the spiritual ruler of mankind and to bend history to His purpose, is hanging on it still. That is His victory and His reign.'[9]

Although Schweitzer's views, as set forth in *The Quest of the Historical Jesus* and subsequent writings, have more often met with dissent than acceptance, their influence in focusing attention upon the eschatology of the Gospels is still dominant. In this country, the late Professor F. C. Burkitt became a devoted disciple. In the second edition of *The Gospel History and its Transmission*, published in 1907, while there is an isolated reference in the Preface to Schweitzer's 'admirable history of the attempts to write a life of Jesus', Burkitt is simply concerned to commend his critical estimate of Bruno Bauer's historical scepticism. In 1909, however, the essay which he contributed to a volume edited by Swete indicated a marked movement in the direction of Schweitzer's thoroughgoing eschatology, and in the essay published in *A History of Christianity in the Light of Modern Knowledge* (1929, Part II, p. 234) he is so far in agreement with Schweitzer as to be able to write: 'What I think certain is that Jesus was fully persuaded that, unless He did of His own initiative court failure and a violent death, the new state of things so ardently expected and longed for would not arrive.'

Among other writers whose approach was deeply affected by Schweitzer's work were Sanday, E. F. Scott, Moffatt, and Streeter. Sanday, who introduced with some enthusiasm Schweitzer's views to English theology before the translation of *The Quest of the Historical Jesus* appeared, became less cordial in his support by 1911, as his article in the *Hibbert Journal* in October of that year indicates. *The Kingdom and Messiah* (1911) by E. F. Scott and Moffatt's *Theology of the Gospels* (1912) bear unmistakable signs of the new era in New Testament studies that had dawned, although both writers, while recognizing that the eschatological element was of fundamental importance, were aware of the inadequacy of the theory of thoroughgoing eschatology. Streeter, in an

[9] op. cit. (E.T., 2nd edn.), p. 369.

appendix to *Oxford Studies in the Synoptic Problem* (1911), deals briefly with the tendency for the eschatological language of Christ to be conformed in some Gospel documents to the apocalyptic picture cherished in the early Church—a theme which was considered by von Dobschütz in *The Eschatology of the Gospels* (1910). In his essay in *Foundations* (1912) on 'The Historic Christ', Streeter has obviously come under the sway for the time being of Schweitzer, but his subsequent writings suggest that, sympathetic as he was to every new interpretation in religious thought, he came to modify his position.

The eschatological theory was in some quarters rejected outright or completely ignored. Wellhausen[10] held that the mind of Jesus reflected the eternal relations of God and man, and that He dissociated Himself from the expectations of His time. Unfortunately, the Church saw in Daniel 7[13] ('I saw . . . one like the Son of man') a prophecy of Christ, and after His death His person became associated with apocalyptic hopes. The apocalyptic elements are thus excluded from the teaching of Christ, and attributed to the erroneous identification by the Apostolic Church of the person of Christ with the Son of Man in Daniel.

In England, T. R. Glover's *Jesus of History* was published in 1917, and though it was not intended to rank as a work of technical scholarship, no book of its time had a more potent influence upon the religious outlook of men and women, young and old, throughout the world. If today it seems remote in spite of its incomparable picture of the humanity of Jesus, the reason is partly to be sought in its complete indifference to the eschatological framework of the Gospels. Again, Cyril Emmett, who with Lily Dougall wrote *Lord of Thought* (1922), contended that the teaching of Jesus about the fatherly love of God could not be reconciled with the alleged eschatological passages in the Gospels and presented us with a view of Jesus which involved a repudiation of the eschatological setting.

Some of the more representative interpretations of the Kingdom of God in the teaching of Jesus which have appeared within the last quarter of the present century may now be reviewed. Common to them all is the conviction that however unsatisfactory Schweitzer's futurist eschatology may be, the teaching of Jesus cannot be isolated from its eschatological context.

[10] *Introduction to the First Three Gospels* (2nd edn. 1911).

INTRODUCTION 17

We turn first to *Reich Gottes und Kirche im Neuen Testament* (*The Kingdom of God and the Church in the New Testament*) by Gerhard Gloege, published in 1929. The importance of Gloege's work lies in his careful examination of the biblical conception of the Kingdom of God, his emphasis upon the Kingdom as a divine intervention or 'miracle' present in the Person and Works of Jesus, and his treatment of the relation between the Kingdom and the Church. Following upon the labours of Dalman (*The Words of Jesus*, 1902) and supported later in his conclusions by Karl Ludwig Schmidt[11] and many other scholars, he shows that the biblical conception of the Kingdom is the kingly Rule of God. It is not a product of human effort or natural evolution, but a divine act explicable only by reference to the dynamic activity of God. From one point of view the Kingdom is beyond time and its reality is unaffected by human response. Nevertheless it is related to time, since it is present 'with power' in the world, opposed though it is to the existing order, and it will find its consummation in the fulfilment of God's redemptive purpose which is the end of divine activity. The future age or the 'endtime' has broken into the present world in the Words and Works of Jesus, in whose activity we see the activity of God Himself. Through Jesus, the Christ of God, divine forgiveness and lifegiving power are brought to men—a certain sign of the advent of the Messianic Age. When Gloege comes to an examination of the relation of the Church to the Kingdom, he shows that the Church is not to be regarded either as synonymous with the Kingdom or as a substitute for it. The 'ecclesia' is the new people of God, the organ of the divine Will, and it owes its origin and existence to the kingly Rule of God. Since God works in the Church by His Spirit, the Church is above the world, yet active within it as the channel of His reconciling purpose, and looks to the day when God shall be all in all.

The dynamic view of the Kingdom of God so vigorously and convincingly expounded by Gloege finds expression in another great work of this period, *The Kingdom of God and the Son of Man*, by Rudolph Otto (E.T., 1938; first published in German edition, 1934).

It is difficult to attach a label to Otto's view of the Kingdom of God, and the common term 'anticipated eschatology' is somewhat

[11] *Kittel Theologisches Wörterbuch* (Art., '*Basileus*', etc.).

misleading. While Otto holds that the Kingdom in the Gospels is not wholly present, his central conception is that it is manifested in the Person and Work of Jesus. He dissents from the belief that Jesus brings the Kingdom. On the contrary, he declares, the Kingdom brings Him with it. Jesus was not a mere eschatological preacher; 'rather His person and work were part of a comprehensive redemptive event, which broke in with Him and which He called the coming and actual arrival of the Kingdom of God' (p. 104). And the Kingdom comes chiefly not as claim and decision, but as redeeming power to set free a demon-ridden world. Jesus knew Himself to be a part and an organ of the eschatological order, and the discipleship which He demanded was not the kind of adherence required by rabbis, but commitment to 'the soteriological and eschatological saviour'. This conception of Jesus as the dynamic Saviour who manifests in His actions the inbreaking divine power is interpreted in relation to the concept of the Son of Man in 1 Enoch, which Otto, on grounds widely considered to be inadequate, regards as central to the Book of Enoch as a whole and as holding the key to the story of Jesus. The highly debatable inferences from the Book of Enoch do not, however, affect his conclusion that Jesus conceived of His death as that of the Messiah-designate and that, in the belief which He held about His own Person, there is a clear synthesis of the Son of Man and Isaiah's servant of God (p. 252), which is brought to a climax in the Last Supper. At the Supper, He gave His disciples a share in His suffering as Servant of God and so bequeathed to them His own inheritance of the Kingdom. The essential point of Christ's action in the rite was the inheritance of the Kingdom of God, and he contends that forgiveness and expiation were not the end, but the means to the final goal, means whereby men might enter into God's Kingdom (p. 311).

The conception of the Kingdom as present in the Person and Work of Jesus is carried a stage farther in the writings of Professor C. H. Dodd.[12] He reminds us that the coming of the Kingdom of God in judgement and redemptive power was an essential element in the Jewish eschatological hope which enabled the Jewish people to weather the storm of suffering and persecution. The proclamation, 'The Kingdom of God has come upon you', broke

[12] *The Parables of the Kingdom* (1935), *The Apostolic Preaching and its Developments* (1936), *History and the Gospel* (1938), etc.

up the scheme of Jewish apocalypse, and what had been an object of hope was now, at any rate in part, a realized experience. The kingdom has come—not has drawn near or is upon the threshold—in the person of the Messiah. Jesus uses the title 'Son of Man', which suggests that in His life of service, His passion, His death, the powers of the Kingdom are liberated and that beyond death He will reign as Lord of a redeemed humanity. The prophets until John looked for the inauguration of God's kingdom; His own disciples enjoy privileges which the prophets of the Old Testament had been denied. Something greater than Solomon is here. What, then, does Professor Dodd make of the sayings about the future Kingdom and of many of the parables which seem to speak of judgement and a consummation in the future? He urges in regard to these sayings that, in the formation of the Gospel tradition, the eschatological elements suffered expansion; that predictions belonging to different planes of thought became confused; and that the best attested among the various predictions are symbolic and refer to realities transcending history. 'These future tenses are only an accommodation of language. There is no coming of the Son of Man "after" His coming in Galilee and Jerusalem whether soon or late, for there is no before or after in the eternal order' (*Parables of the Kingdom*, p. 108). It should perhaps be noted that in his small book *The Coming of Christ* (1951) there appears to be some modification of this position. When we turn to the parables, we are reminded of the importance of their setting in life, and that setting, according to Professor Dodd, is to be found not in the life of the Apostolic Church but in the life of Jesus Himself. Parables of judgement are thus taken to refer to the crisis which the inauguration of the Kingdom has already created and parables of growth are to be interpreted in relation to the fields that are already white to harvest. The development is in the past. A long process has ripened into a crisis. Zero-hour has already arrived and it demands a decision.

It would appear from this brief survey of representative works that the field of study to which they belong has been well ploughed. Of the writing of books on the Kingdom of God in the Gospels there would seem to be no end, and few, if any, recent publications succeed in raising issues which have not been explored by leading

New Testament scholars. Indeed it is doubtful whether much fresh light may be expected to dawn from further linguistic and exegetical study of the subject or from a wider acquaintance with the Old Testament and the Jewish and pagan background in the first century. The time seems to have come, first, to inquire whether it is possible to give a constructive account of the teaching of Jesus about the Kingdom as found in the Synoptic Gospels on the basis of recent studies, even if much is hidden from us and many controversial questions remain unanswered, and secondly, to examine the theological implications of the teaching of Jesus about the Kingdom and consider whether they can be so interpreted as to constitute a theology that is systematic and distinctive. We shall hope to show that the Kingdom as conceived by Jesus presupposes a doctrine of God, the Person and Work of Christ, the Church, and Eternal Hope. Theology and ethics are interwoven in the teaching of Jesus and if it is thought that insufficient attention has been given in our discussion to the ethics of the Kingdom, the reason lies in the necessary delimitation of our study. The ethical implications of the teaching of Jesus about the Kingdom call for a separate work.

The eschatological interpretation of the New Testament is a familiar enough conception among biblical scholars of all schools. It has yet to reach the non-specialist in the churches and without. Unless it can be built up into the preaching, worship, life and thought of the Church as a whole, there is little ground for hope that it will prove to be anything but a passing phase in Christian thought. What finally determines the general acceptance of a fresh orientation of the Gospel is not the evidence amassed by scholars which they alone can assess, but the degree to which it can be appropriated by the Christian believer. If the eschatological approach to the Gospel can be assimilated by those who have been nurtured in the Christian Faith by Word and Sacrament, then it may well prove to be the birth of a new epoch, not only in theological thought, but in the faith and life of the Christian community.

CHAPTER ONE

THE KINGDOM OF GOD IN THE TEACHING OF JESUS

JESUS presupposed the Old Testament and any approach to the understanding of the teaching of Jesus about the Kingdom of God must take the Old Testament as its starting-point. The actual term 'Kingdom of God' does not occur in the Old Testament, but the idea of the Kingdom is central to its thought (cf. Ps 22^{28}, 103^{19}, 145^{13}, 1 Ch 29^{11}, Dn 7$^{27ff.}$). Its meaning there is the kingship of God—never a kingdom in the sense of a territory, or an association of human beings. The Kingdom is, in fact, rooted in the conception of God as King. For the Hebrews there can only be one king over Israel and, as at a later stage they came to see, there can only be one king over the whole world, even if He appoints His deputies who may or may not obey His will. God is eternally King. Man cannot make Him king or dislodge Him from His throne. But the Kingdom of God in the Old Testament is also future. The prophets were preachers to their own day, and it is important that we should recognize that their message was conditioned by the contemporary scene. If, however, the element of prediction in prophecy is ignored, or at any rate regarded as incidental, we shall fail to do full justice to the prophets as preachers to their contemporaries. It was an integral part of their message since they were concerned not only with the immediate future and the inevitable consequences of policies which were at variance with the Rule of God, but with the dawn of a new order or age. Beyond the working-out in sorrow, suffering and disaster of the rebellion of man against God, they saw the coming of the Kingdom of God. This consummation is not causally connected with previous events. That is, the new age is not conceived as growing out of the present by a natural evolution or by human effort. It is of God, Who alone can bring it to pass. The great 'Day of the Lord' is different from every other day, for it is the final term which gives meaning to the whole series. The sovereignty of God, so often veiled by the seeming triumph of evil and the betrayals even of the people of God, will be finally manifested, and the entire historical process will be summed up in the triumphant revelation of divine righteousness. There are many pictures given of the age that is to come, and though some are associated with a divine leader, others contain no reference to the Messiah. Nevertheless, in spite of the various forms under which the hope of the distant future appears in Isaiah, Micah, Jeremiah, and Daniel, there is a striking unanimity among the various predictions. The Age to Come is to be set up not by man but by God. It will bring peace and concord springing from obedience to the will of God. The reign of evil will give place to the righteous reign of God. Nature itself will be transformed. The wolf shall dwell with the lamb and the leopard shall lie down with the kid. Behind this prophecy of Isaiah (11ff.) is the conviction, which has sometimes been too readily dismissed, that the cruelty of nature is to be traced to the kingdom of evil which has infected nature, animal life, and human beings.

The conception of the new age was elaborated with the aid of strange imagery in the apocalyptic literature which belongs approximately to the last two centuries B.C. and the first century A.D. This literature is chiefly represented in the Bible by Isaiah 24–27, the Book of Daniel and the Book of Revelation. Outside the canonical Scriptures, the most important apocalyptic writings are those ascribed to Enoch and Baruch, the *Testaments of the Twelve Patriarchs* and 4 Ezra. While the distinction between prophetic and apocalyptic eschatology must not be too sharply drawn, the primary interest of apocalyptic is in the age beyond, which cannot be described in terms of normal human experience and which is discontinuous with what has gone before. Its main concern is with the Kingdom in another world or age, rather than with the prophetic concept of the Kingdom to be established in this world. Apocalypsis thus means the revealing of secrets to the elect about this other world, and about what is happening there now, as well as what will happen when the heavenly kingdom by supernatural action breaks into the historical process and brings the present age to an end. The distinction between the present age and the age to come is thus central in the apocalyptic literature. But there is another dualism which is inseparable from the concept of the two ages. It is found in the conflict between the Kingdom of God and the kingdom of evil. There is no warrant for supposing that the apocalyptic writers conceived of two co-eternal powers struggling for supremacy. Victory lies with God, for He alone is eternal. Evil inheres in created beings, incarnate or discarnate, and in spite of their disobedience and rebellion they are under divine control. But there is a kingdom of evil powerfully organized, and its baneful influence penetrates the world of nature and man. In the present age it seems to be in the ascendant, but the sufferings and disasters which are mounting with such rapidity to the utter consternation of the faithful are signs of the approaching end. Evil exists to be destroyed and the day of judgement and deliverance is at hand. 'And then His kingdom shall appear throughout all His creation and then Satan shall be no more' (*Assumption of Moses* 10^1).

There are varying descriptions of the Kingdom in this literature. Sometimes it is conceived as a kingdom on this earth, but sometimes as having its home on a new earth or in another world. Sometimes, the coming of the Kingdom is associated with the figure of a Messiah or the saints of the Most High. Sometimes, as in the *Assumption of Moses*, the Kingdom is established by the direct intervention of God without any mediator. There are, again, differing views about the duration of the Messianic Kingdom on this earth, and there are those who look only to the establishment of the eternal Kingdom in heaven. Common to all the Apocalyptists is the conviction that at the end of history there will be Judgement to which all men and nations must submit.

Although we look in vain for a consistent picture of the Kingdom of God in the Apocalyptic writings, there is one conviction underlying the varieties of form which have been noted. The Kingdom is the Kingdom of God. In the present age and in that which is to come God rules. The first and last word in history is with Him.

It is not possible for us to determine with precision the teaching of the Rabbis at the beginning of the Christian era about the Messianic Hope in the wider sense of a Golden Age, since the literature at our disposal belongs to a later date. While they looked forward to the final overthrow of evil and the consummation of the reign of God, they were probably concerned less, before the destruction of the Temple and Jewish State, with Messianic hopes than with the Kingdom of God as a divine discipline. In the Rabbinic literature the Kingdom of God means, not the sphere which is governed by Him,[1] but the kingship or rule of God. Hence the Rabbis teach the duty of taking the yoke of the Kingdom of God upon oneself by a confession of belief in the unity of God and a wholehearted submission to the Mosaic Law. 'If you have taken my Kingdom upon you, take also my commandments: Thou shalt have no other God but me.' These and similar expressions make it clear that the Kingdom is not conceived as a State or empire or political organization, but as the Sovereign Rule of God to which man owes undivided allegiance.

The Kingdom of God in Hebrew literature means primarily the kingship or the Sovereign Rule of God. Its nature is determined by the character of God as personal and 'dynamic'. Perhaps we come nearer to the Hebrew conception of the Kingdom when we think not so much of the Rule of God, which can easily become an abstract idea, but of God ruling, God accomplishing His unchanging purpose of redemption in accordance with His righteous will. The Kingdom of God in the Old Testament and later Jewish literature is thus an eschatological idea, by which we mean that the activity of God throughout the whole of history is governed by the End, or the eternal purpose which is to be fulfilled in the future. Eternity and Time are not antithetical in Hebrew thought. Time is the medium through which the eternal purpose of God is manifested. God, that is, reveals His Rule through the medium of events, and revelation waits upon divine events. 'I will be what I will be' (Ex 3¹⁴)—the answer which Moses receives when he asks to be told God's name—is not a metaphysical statement about the nature of God, but a declaration that God cannot be known until He has taken action. He went into action when He delivered the Hebrews from Egypt, and in the institution of the covenant which He made with them we have a partial revelation of the divine Rule which is present and future. The Rule of God is already manifest in the history and religion of the Hebrew people, for if the main theme of the Old Testament is the Rule of God, that Rule implies the people of God, who were called to interpret its meaning to the world and to witness through loyalty to the divine Law the fulfilment of its promises. At the end of history or the present historical process, it was believed that God, whose hand can be

[1] *Theol. Wort. Kuhn*, I.570.

traced from creation onward and particularly in certain historical events in which His judgement and mercy are transparent to those who have eyes to see, would bring His kingdom in. On that day not only would His goodness be known, but it would be given to men to behold His glory.

We now turn to the teaching of Jesus about the Kingdom of God, as found in the Synoptic Gospels. There seems to be wide agreement among our authorities that the Greek word '*Basileia*', which represents the Aramaic word '*malkuth*' used probably by Jesus, means kingship, and that its primary reference in the sayings and parables of Jesus is to the sovereign rule of God rather than to the community or realm over which He reigns. Dr. Vincent Taylor[2] has reminded us that if we examine the sixty sayings and parables in which Jesus speaks of the *Basileia* and exclude parallel versions of the same saying, in less than a sixth of them is the thought of a community either distinctive or prominent. In the overwhelming majority, the central thought is the Rule of God. As will soon become evident, the idea of kingship implies realm, since rule or reign could have no intelligible meaning apart from persons who are ruled, and though the Kingdom of God is not constituted by the community, its significance cannot be understood when it is taken out of relation to the community.

The Kingdom of God was the theme of our Lord's teaching, as of His life, death, and resurrection. We speak of parables of the Kingdom and it may be convenient so to classify certain parables. But all the parables of Jesus were parables of the Kingdom and all His sayings were expositions of the Rule of God. What then did our Lord teach about the Kingdom, the rule or reign of God?

(1) *The Kingdom is the Rule of Grace*

One of the most characteristic sayings of Jesus is the injunction to love our enemies, and let it be said that what signifies in assessing the importance of any saying is not whether it is original, but whether it is characteristic of the teaching as a whole. 'Ye have heard that it was said, Thou shalt love thy neighbour, and

[2] *Jesus and His Sacrifice* (1937), pp. 8ff.

hate thine enemy: but I say unto you, Love your enemies, and pray for them that persecute you; that ye may be sons of your Father which is in heaven: for he maketh his sun to rise on the evil and the good, and sendeth rain on the just and the unjust' (Mt 5:43-5; cf. Lk 6:27-8, 32-6).

Here it is clearly implied that God's dealings with men are not determined by merit and that His grace cannot be earned. And the saying does not stand alone. Jesus speaks of the sower sowing seed almost indiscriminately—some fell by the wayside, some on stony ground, some among thorns. There is inevitable waste, but waste is one of the risks of love. We have again the parable of the labourers in the vineyard (Mt 20:1-16). The sympathy of many who would regard themselves as 'good Christians' is with the labourers who had borne the heat and burden of the day and who complained that they had been unjustly treated. Certainly the contrast between generally accepted canons of justice and the rule of God is set in bold relief, and the parable illustrates the text: 'For as the heavens are higher than the earth, so are my ways higher than your ways, and my thoughts than your thoughts' (Is 55:9). A principle of action which seems to be singularly inapposite in the routine of commercial life is nevertheless widely adopted in the family, where the youngest is not penalized because he is the last to arrive. Within the family circle, rewards are not in exact proportion to service rendered. Love which disdains to count the cost is the law of family life and it brooks no rival.

It is this central emphasis upon the unrestricted love of God which enables us to understand in a measure the nature of our Lord's conflict with the Pharisees. The picture given in the Synoptic Gospels of the Pharisees has caused misgiving not only among Jewish scholars but among Christians, although it should be noted that not all Jewish scholars are agreed that it is unjust.[3] Obviously you cannot indict a whole sect, and there were doubtless Pharisees who were not meant to be included in the severity of our Lord's condemnation. But the fact remains that the Pharisaic system, even when it was free from the taint of spurious piety and blatant hypocrisy, was diametrically opposed to God's Rule of Grace which Jesus sought to commend. It rested upon

---

[3] cf. C. Anderson Scott, *New Testament Ethics* (1934), pp. 40ff. F. B. Clogg, *The Christian Character in the Early Church* (1944), pp. 101ff.

the belief that it is possible for a man to make himself fit to have fellowship with God and that it is within his power by obedience to the law to win His favour. Hence there were those Pharisees —and there is reason to believe that they were a considerable body—who went beyond the requirements of the law in order to store up merit and establish a claim upon God. Such an attitude, illustrated with piercing relevance in the story of the Pharisee and the publican at prayer (Lk 18⁹⁻¹⁴), produces a type of character marked by self-righteousness and self-deception, and has its nemesis in self-exclusion from the kingdom of grace.

Although there may be little disposition to defend the products of the Pharisaic system, the doctrine of the indiscriminate and unrestricted grace of God sometimes creates difficulties, particularly for those who are concerned that no conception of God should be entertained which seems to threaten the sanctity of the Moral Law. At first sight, it would appear that the authority of the Moral Law is abrogated by the Rule of Grace, but closer consideration suggests that there is no contradiction between Law and Love.

(i) Grace is not the denial of the Moral Law, but its fulfilment. Justice is giving what is due. We may ask what is God's due if He is our Father, and what is our neighbour's due, or that of our enemy, if we are all children of God? There is no room within the family of God for claims and counterclaims. Those who are under the Rule of Grace will certainly love their neighbour, but they will go farther and love their enemy. Every situation will constitute an opportunity for the imitation of the benevolence of God. When we have faithfully fulfilled the strict requirements of the Moral Law, grace will still condemn us as unprofitable servants, unless we are prepared to respond to its infinite demands.

(ii) It is only in a universe which has unrestricted love as its foundation that we can learn to seek goodness for its own sake. The Moral Law is associated with rewards and punishments, and these have their place in the development of human character. When, however, the thought of reward and punishment becomes dominant, it may strengthen self-centredness rather than foster a disinterested pursuit of virtue. If there were a point-to-point correspondence between virtue and happiness on the one hand,

and wickedness and misery on the other, wickedness might disappear or be reduced, but so would virtue. When justice is raised to the level of love, it banishes self-interest and awakens what is akin to itself. Love begets love.

(iii) The Rule of Grace presupposes judgement upon self-centredness in all its forms. It is no accident that Jesus, who proclaimed the Rule of Grace, should have widened the area of penitence so as to include attitudes of mind such as the unforgiving spirit, unbrotherliness, contempt, and censoriousness, which were considered to be quite compatible with allegiance to the Moral Law. He tracked sin down from its outward expression in conduct to the underlying motive which often lay concealed beneath respectable morality, good works and fervent piety.

(iv) Grace or unrestricted love creates its own demands. Jesus offered to men life under the rule of divine grace, but those who accepted the offer found themselves confronted by an absolute demand. In all circumstances they are to love God with their whole being and their neighbour as themselves. There can be no doubt that a primary place is given to the family in the ethical teaching of Jesus (Mk 7^{9-13}, 10^{2-12}; Mt 5^{32}; Lk 16^{18}), but it may prove necessary to renounce family ties in loyalty to the Kingdom of God (Mk 10^{29}; Mt 10^{35}; Lk 12^{53}). If the body proves a hindrance to the service of God through its insistent demands and tyrannical sway, the most rigorous and costly discipline must be exercised. Where the hands, the feet and the eyes constantly resist control, it is better that they should be put out of action than that we should be shut out of the Kingdom of God (Mt 18^{8-9}; Mk 9^{43-7}). To be a disciple of Jesus is to take up the cross, and that means blotting yourself out. This act of complete self-renunciation is seen in the forgiving spirit, infinite compassion, unfailing humility and indomitable courage. Perhaps the most exacting demand which Jesus made was that we should become as little children (Mk 10^{15})[4]—an affront to an age which is confident that it can work out its own salvation. To become as a little child in our relation to God is to recognize our dependence upon Him, to know His love for us and our love for Him, and to realize that without Him we are undone. It is to know the meaning of simple trust in a world that is laden with

[4] cf. R. N. Flew, *The Idea of Perfection in Christian Theology* (1934), p. 10.

unknown perils. It is to have the assurance that because we have committed ourselves to Him He will take charge of our situation and keep us secure. 'Nothing in my hand I bring.' How few of us have reached that mature stage of Christian experience which enables us to receive the Kingdom of God as a little child!

The gift of life in the Kingdom creates its own peculiar demands and makes possible their fulfilment, so that the Kingdom, as gift and demand, is all of God.

We have spoken of the Rule of God as the Rule of Grace, but all static and legal conceptions of grace are utterly foreign to the teaching of Jesus about God's Rule. Grace is the personal activity of God governed throughout by His unchanging purpose of redemptive love for man. In the fulfilment of that purpose God takes the initiative, and thus the Kingdom of God is set before us not as a human achievement but as the gift of God. It is God Himself going into action in a world dominated by evil powers to secure the victory of love, and the subjugation of demons by Jesus and His disciples is a sign of the beginning of the end (Lk 10[18]; Mt 12[28]). The battleground is the world, and the Kingdom is to come on earth as it is in heaven.

(2) *The Kingdom of God is present in Jesus*

The coming of the Kingdom of God in judgement and mercy was an essential feature of Hebrew religion. In spite of suffering and persecution, the hope was invincible that God would intervene and visit and redeem His people. It was the message of Jesus that the Kingdom had come and that the day which generations had longed to see had dawned. The evidence that Jesus taught that the Kingdom was a present reality, not only in the sense that it is always present because it is the eternal rule of God, but that God Himself had taken redemptive action and revealed His rule in the Person and Work of Christ, has been forcibly presented in recent works—notably by Otto in *The Kingdom of God and the Son of Man* and Professor Dodd in *The Parables of the Kingdom* and other works. It is therefore not necessary to do more than refer to certain passages which imply that in the mind of Jesus the rule of sovereign love, or the Kingdom of God, had broken into human life, and that God had in Jesus taken unique and decisive action. 'The time is fulfilled,' said

Jesus, 'and the kingdom of God is at hand: repent ye, and believe the Gospel' (Mk 1[15]). Again, in Lk 11[20] (Mt 12[28]), we have the saying: 'If I by the finger of God cast out devils, then is the kingdom of God come upon you.' There has been, and still is, some dispute as to whether the Greek verbs in the above passages (*'eggiken'*, translated 'is at hand', in the former, and *'ephthasen'*, in the latter, translated 'come upon you') are capable of being interpreted as meaning that the Kingdom is a present reality, or whether the element of anticipation still clings to them. (cf. e.g. *Expository Times*, XLVIII 91-4, in which Professor Dodd's view is challenged.) Whatever may be said about the evidence adduced from the Septuagint usage and modern colloquial Greek, the preceding phrase in the Marcan passage, 'The time is fulfilled', and other sayings which imply that the Kingdom is a present reality, point to the meaning 'has come'. In the charge to his disciples, Jesus says: 'Into whatsoever city ye enter . . . heal the sick that are therein, and say unto them, The kingdom of God is come nigh unto you' (Lk 10[8-9]; Mt 10[7]). 'Blessed are the eyes which see the things that ye see: for I say unto you, that many prophets and kings desired to see the things which ye see, and saw them not; and to hear the things which ye hear, and heard them not' (Lk 10[23f.], Mt 13[16f.]). In answer to John the Baptist's question (Mt 11[2-11], Lk 7[18-30]) the signs that were expected to accompany the coming of the Kingdom are named and the inference is that there is no need to look for 'another'. 'A greater than Solomon is here' (Lk 11[31f.]; Mt 12[41f.]).

The teaching of these passages is reinforced by the place given to works of healing and other miraculous events in the Synoptic record. They are manifestations of the Rule of God in action and indicate that the coming of the Kingdom means victory over the powers of evil which have invaded life at every level. The attempts to isolate the miracles from the framework of our Lord's ministry and to treat them as Hellenistic wonder stories, or in the case of the healing miracles as anticipations of modern psychotherapy, cannot be sustained. Whatever may be the verdict upon the authenticity of this or that miracle, the miracles are an integral part of the Synoptic account of the life and work of Jesus and are there regarded as expressions of the redemptive rule of God.

Again, Jesus associated the Kingdom with His own person.

THE KINGDOM OF GOD IN THE TEACHING OF JESUS

The famous saying 'All things have been delivered unto me of my Father: and no one knoweth the Son, save the Father; neither doth any know the Father, save the Son, and he to whomsoever the Son willeth to reveal Him' (Mt 11^{27}), has often been questioned on insufficient grounds—its kinship to sayings in the Fourth Gospel and its seemingly metaphysical character. What we have in these words is an unreasoned statement which unveils our Lord's filial consciousness. He conceived Himself to be in a unique relation to God and His Rule. He never sets Himself side by side with man in His approach to God. In the Lord's prayer, we have the words 'Our Father' but the prayer was His response to the request for instruction as to the way to pray— 'When ye pray, say'. Jesus experienced loneliness, not because He sought it, nor chiefly because He was opposed and wantonly misunderstood, but because He had a unique relation to God which carried with it a unique task.

This unique relationship with God and His kingdom is focused in the use of the title 'Son of Man'. There is little if any room for doubt that Jesus used the title 'Son of Man' in most cases of Himself, and that whether we translate the phrase He uses as 'Son of Man' or 'Man' it held for him a distinctive meaning. The figure of the 'Son of Man' may be traced to the idea of a primal or heavenly man found in oriental mythology and appropriated by Jewish apocalyptic. The direct source of the title as used by Jesus was probably the Book of Daniel rather than the Similitudes of Enoch (*Enoch* 37–71), since both the date and the uncertainty whether our Lord was familiar with the document make it difficult to entertain the view that he derived it from Enoch. That Jesus was familiar with the *Book of Daniel* is not disputed and the relevant passage is Daniel 7$^{13-14}$: 'I saw in the night visions, and, behold, there came with the clouds of heaven one like unto a son of man. . . . And there was given him dominion, and glory, and a kingdom.' But as is evident from 7^{18} and 7^{27}, the 'one like unto a son of man' represents the saints of the Most High, the faithful remnant of the Jewish race, although if the title were removed from its context in Daniel it would most naturally suggest the picture of an individual, as it does in Enoch.

While the debate as to the origin and significance of the term 'Son of Man' still proceeds, it is the meaning of the term as used by Jesus that matters, since his treatment of traditional sources was governed by the consciousness of His vocation. The title appears in three different types of sayings: those of a general character such as 'The Son of man is come eating and drinking' (Lk 7[34]) and 'The Son of man hath not where to lay his head' (Lk 9[58]); those which refer to the Messianic glory and the Parousia; and those which relate to suffering and death, in which the august figure of the Son of Man is united with the figure of the Suffering Servant.

Many differing interpretations have been suggested. It has been argued that the title means 'Messiah-designate', since Jesus could not be revealed as Messiah until His exaltation. The weakness of this view is that the title is used as noted above in Parousia sayings. The same objection may be lodged against the popular interpretation of the use of the title as descriptive of our Lord's human nature. T. W. Manson's suggestion[5] that 'Son of Man' should be interpreted corporately so as to include Jesus and His disciples has won some support, but while the concept of corporate personality central to Hebrew thought has its place in the teaching of Jesus, no passage in the Gospels requires this theory and there are few passages in which it yields a wholly satisfactory interpretation. It should be added that Professor Manson admits that when it becomes apparent that not even the disciples are ready to rise to the demands of the ideal, Jesus stands alone, 'embodying in His own person the perfect human response to the regal claims of God'.[6]

We may perhaps conclude that Jesus used this title (which, except in Acts 7[56], does not occur in the New Testament outside the Gospels, where it is used freely by Jesus in the latter part of His ministry) to express the conviction that He was God's Messiah, called to walk with sinful men, bearing the burden of their sin and shame, to offer to them the blessings of the divine rule, and to enter upon the kingship which He was to receive from the Father by treading the path of humiliation and death. The ideas of exaltation and obedience unto death are brought together in this mysterious title which was free from certain features in the current conceptions of the Messiah which Jesus rejected. There was about Him a Messianic reserve, not only because false notions of the Messiah were abroad, but because His work was yet to be completed. He thus avoided the open

---

[5] *The Teaching of Jesus* (1931), pp. 211-36.   [6] ibid., p. 228.

assertion of Messiahship during His ministry. The term 'Son of Man' served His purpose, and with characteristic freedom He employed it to set forth the task which He had been called to discharge as the divine agent of the Rule of God. The conception of the Kingdom of God is thereby linked with that of the coming of the Son of Man. In His complete obedience to the divine will, consummated in His humiliation and death, the eternal Kingdom has come, and the purpose of God for mankind has been unveiled once and for all time.

(3) *The Kingdom of God in the teaching of Jesus implies a future consummation*

In the teaching of Jesus about the Kingdom of God there are sayings about what is to come to pass after His death which have given rise to vigorous controversy (Mk $10^{39\text{ff.}}$, 13^{11-13}; Lk $14^{26\text{f.}}$= Mt $10^{37\text{ff.}}$; Lk 13^{35}=Mt 23^{38}; Lk 19^{41-4}; Lk 11^{49-51}=Mt 23^{34-6}). Some scholars seem to be able to rest in the view that Jesus believed that His resurrection would be followed almost immediately by the winding-up of history and the end of the world. Among the considerations which rule out that unduly simplified version, there are, first, the warnings given to his disciples about the sufferings that await them and the predictions about the downfall of Jerusalem and the destruction of the Temple. These disasters cannot be explained as 'prophecies after the event', and their incidence requires the continuance of history, at least for a period. Secondly, the ethical teaching of Jesus is related to life in this world and not to an ideal society. The 'Sermon on the Mount' would be irrelevant in a society in which all live by the rule of love. Unless history is to continue, the teaching of Jesus with its universal emphasis seems singularly out of place. The ethics of Jesus which are concerned with human relations in society become unintelligible if it is assumed that He envisaged a speedy close to the existing order. Then there are the parables of growth (the sower, the mustard seed, the wheat and tares) and what have been described as the parables of effort (the pearl of great price, the talents), which have as their most natural setting the kingdom as future in time as well as present, rather than the conditions of our Lord's earthly ministry.

But what are we to infer from the predictions about the

Judgement, the Day of the Son of Man and the coming of the Son of Man in glory?

When sayings upon which a large number of scholars would not rely as evidence are excluded, there is a sufficient number left to indicate that the idea of future judgement was an integral element in the teaching of Jesus and that He believed it was to be associated with His person (Mk 8^{38}=Mt 10^{33}; Lk 12^9, and the allegory of the Sheep and the Goats, in Mt $25^{31\text{ff.}}$, which should be handled with caution). While the judgement lies beyond the present order, human accountability is here represented as determined by the attitude of man to the revelation of the Rule of God in Jesus, and the Fourth Evangelist has made central what is implicit in the Synoptic Gospels. But 'realized judgement' does not exhaust the teaching of Jesus and, if much remains undisclosed, the prominence given to judgement beyond history as at present known cannot be ignored.

In regard to sayings about the coming of the Son of Man, it must be recognized that they cannot be reduced to a logical scheme. The mythology of Jewish apocalyptic is employed and we must beware of assuming that we can speak with confidence of the interpretation which was placed upon the imagery used by Jesus. As we trace the tradition from Matthew through Mark and Q to such a reconstruction of oral tradition as is possible, the prominence given to the allusions about the coming of the Son of Man seems to recede. But again it is vain to pass over lightly the idea of the glory to follow which is unmistakably represented in the Gospel tradition, or to regard the Resurrection and the coming of the Son of Man as alternative expressions even if there is no saying available which predicts both. The sayings about the coming of the Son of Man imply a far more inclusive idea.

There are at least a few well attested sayings (Lk 12^{40}, $17^{22, 26, 30}$, 18^{8b}, Mk 14^{62}). Of these the most significant is the Marcan saying. 'Art thou the Messiah?' Jesus is asked, and the answer comes swiftly: 'I am: and ye shall see the Son of man sitting at the right hand of power, and coming with the clouds of heaven.' The language comes from Daniel 7^{13} and Psalm 110^1. The 'beasts' in Daniel are the pagan empires, and the Son of man represents the people of the saints of the Most High who are to take the place of authority occupied by the empires of this world. The victory of the saints is to be realized in the establishment of the Kingdom of God on earth. The vision describes a scene in the transcendent sphere, but the symbolism has a corresponding historical reality in the expected sovereignty of the Jewish State. Nothing short of victory amid the very scenes in which the saints had suffered seeming defeat would serve to establish their claim to rule. What precisely should be inferred from 'coming with the clouds of heaven' cannot be determined, but if the passage in Daniel is to be our guide, our Lord's words signify more than a reference to His exaltation to heaven. They imply, as the passage in Daniel implies, that His victory will be registered on earth and His cause vindicated within history.[7]

It is true that Jesus referred to the consummation of the Kingdom in another world where men feast with the blessed dead (Mk 12$^{26f.}$; Mt 8^{11}) and drink new wine in the realm of eternal bliss (Mk 14^{25}). If we take the view that when Jesus spoke of the triumph of the Son of Man He was referring to a timeless fact or a reality transcending history and that the future tenses are an accommodation of language, or that the coming of the Son of Man and the Resurrection refer to the same event—triumph over death and exaltation to heaven—or again that the coming is to be identified with the Spirit, many difficulties are at least mitigated. But we are left with some awkward questions that cannot be evaded. The passages about the future coming of the Son of Man are rooted in the Synoptic tradition and in the faith of the early Church. How was it that the earliest Christians should have so completely misunderstood their Master's meaning?[8] Then, it must be observed that the setting of the teaching of Jesus about the Kingdom is eschatological and must be interpreted in the light of Hebrew rather than Greek thought. For the Hebrew the significant fact is the End to which all things are moving, and while it is true that the Kingdom has come in the life and work of Christ, it cannot be claimed that His victory over sin and death attested by the Resurrection implies the full realization in time of the eternal Rule of God. It can hardly be denied, without ruling out much in the Gospel tradition that may be judged to be authentic and effecting changes in the setting of many of the

[7] It is true that the 'Son of Man' goes to the Ancient of Days and it is not said that he returns to earth.

[8] T. F. Glasson's *The Second Advent* (1945) is an able but unsatisfying treatment of the subject, particularly in its seeming unwillingness to recognize the theological significance of eschatology.

parables, that belief in a decisive event other than the Resurrection or the gift of the Spirit, which would be a final vindication of God's righteousness, was an essential part of the faith of the early Christians, derived from the teaching of their Lord.

(4) *The Kingdom implies communion with God*

The justification of this statement is based upon various strands of evidence.[9] First, there is the teaching about God as Father. 'For him,' writes Professor Manson in a suggestive treatment of the reserve of Jesus in speaking of a familiar conception, 'the Father was the supreme reality in the world and in his own life; and his teaching would make the Father have the same place and power in the life of his disciples, that they too may be heirs, heirs of God and joint-heirs with Jesus Christ.'[10] Further confirmation is found in the teaching about prayer. We are to avoid vain repetitions, since prayer is essentially an act of communion in which we can count on God's unceasing concern for human needs. The language of the Lord's Prayer is the language of fellowship. Out of our fellowship with God comes the desire to do His will and to see His rule finally established on the earth. The petitions about daily bread, forgiveness, and deliverance from such trials as may test our faith to the breaking-point, arise naturally and spontaneously from communion with a loving Father. If Jesus warns us against vain repetitions, he encourages us to practise petition, in which prayer as a personal relation between God and man is so clearly focused. Petitionary prayer implies a sense of dependence upon God, freedom of approach and simple faith in His power and love. These elements are part of the content of the idea of communion with God, and for that reason petitionary prayer should not be regarded as belonging to the lower grades of prayer practised by those who cannot hope to advance to its higher reaches.

Again, the centrality of communion with God as the supreme blessing of the Kingdom is seen in the teaching of Jesus about sin and forgiveness. Sin is a denial of fellowship which is to be traced to a repudiation, conscious or unconscious, of God's Rule of love.

---

[9] cf. A. Raymond George, *Communion with God* (1953), Ch. 2, for a detailed examination of the evidence.

[10] ibid., p. 115.

The list of sins in Mk 7²¹⁻³ is highly significant, since it indicates the things that defile a man in the sense of excluding him from the worship and service of God and from the fellowship of His people. Here is the list: 'Sexual vice, theft, murder, adultery, possessiveness, malice, deceit, wantonness, envying, slander, arrogance, moral obtuseness.'[11] All these sins reveal a disposition to which God is irrevocably opposed. They are sins against God and they block the approaches to His presence. But they are also sins against our fellows. It is in our relations with others that we normally express our relation with God. To sin against our brethren is to sin against our common Father and to exclude us from communion with Him. Similarly the teaching about forgiveness which is so deeply rooted in the Gospel tradition is closely related to the idea of communion with God. The sinner is a debtor and his debt is such that he cannot hope to discharge it in spite of every effort (cf. Mt 18²³⁻⁵; Lk 7⁴¹⁻³). Good works are of no avail, since the wrong is concerned with the inward disposition or the roots of character. He is thus estranged from God and His Rule, and the only remedy for his condition is forgiveness which is a free gift. To be forgiven is to be received back into the fellowship of God, as the parables in Luke 15 indicate. The sinner, however, must repent, although 'repentance' is not to be regarded as merit or as a payment that cancels the debt, but rather as turning away from a life centred in self-interest, in its subtle as well as its blatant forms, to Him who can alone enable us to live in obedience to His Rule of love. It has been observed[12] that when Jesus is actually speaking about God's forgiveness of us, it is not repentance that He mentions; it is our own forgiveness of those who have injured us (Mk 11²⁵; Mt 6¹²ff., 18²³⁻³⁵). But true as this observation is, it must not be understood to mean that the forgiveness of God ceases to be a free gift and is made dependent upon something which man does, as though he must earn the forgiveness of God by forgiving those who have wronged him. What indeed these passages imply is that the unforgiving spirit separates from God and its presence is a sure sign that man has not turned to God. To be ready to forgive is an invariable mark of repentance and of a right relationship to God who is sovereign love.

[11] cf. C. A. Scott, *New Testament Ethics*, pp. 32ff.
[12] W. Temple, *Personal Religion and the Life of Fellowship* (1926), p. 46.

Communion with God is found, as has already become manifest, in the midst of the ordinary relationships of human life. Jesus made extensive use of parables, partly because the knowledge of God is mediated through the created universe—man and nature. It is not possible for God to reveal Himself to man other than through earthly media. To divest ourselves of our normal faculties and to take flight from the world is to open the door to a conception of God which cannot be reconciled with the God and Father of our Lord Jesus Christ. All knowledge of God is mediated, although it is true that the purpose of mediation is to lead us into the immediate presence of God. The media are not, however, cast aside when they have brought us to God, as if they were nothing more than a ladder for which we had no further use. Their significance is gathered up in the experience of God whose nature is revealed within them. Hence, the parables are more than illustrations of our Lord's teaching, since they remind us that God is to be encountered not apart from life but through it. God has left His mark upon nature and human nature, and although evil has obscured the image, it can still be traced. In the ordinary processes of nature and in the spontaneous reactions of men and women, we have some indication of the ways of God with men.

Further, it is significant that the sole absolute command given by our Lord, 'Thou shalt love the Lord thy God . . . and thy neighbour as thyself', links the love of God with the love of our neighbour. Not only is the love we bear to our neighbour the test of the reality of our love to God, but it is through our relations with our neighbour that God comes to us and we come to Him. There is no such thing in the Christian understanding of communion with God as an 'I-Thou' relationship which excludes relationship with others. While it is true that in the teaching of Jesus communion with God is intensely individual, since God is the God of Abraham, Isaac and Jacob, individuality cannot be divorced from its social relations without being emptied of all meaning.

(5) *The Kingdom of God implies a community*

The primary meaning of the Kingdom of God in the Synoptic Gospels is the Rule of God which cannot be identified with the

THE KINGDOM OF GOD IN THE TEACHING OF JESUS

Church as a divine society or with any human organization. Its corporate character, however, is inescapable. The Rule of God is the rule of love and its realization necessarily involves personal relations. Already in other connexions we have seen that the teaching of Jesus about the Kingdom implies a society. What specially concerns us here is the relation of the Kingdom to the Church. The Kingdom is not to be equated with the Church, but it presupposes the Church. In support of this statement, five considerations may be advanced.

(i) The Rule of God is the rule of redemptive love and its end is the gathering of men into its obedience. It thus implies a community of the loyal, the people of God who have taken upon themselves the yoke of the Kingdom. There are passages (Mt 21[31], Lk 16[16]=Mt 11[12f.]; Mk 9[47]) which speak of entering into the Kingdom of God, where kingdom is more naturally translated as sphere or realm. The Kingdom of God and the people of God are correlative terms.

(ii) Some of the parables and metaphors of Jesus suggest a corporate reference. There is for example the parable of the mustard seed (Mk 4[30-2]), which puts out great branches so that the birds of the heaven can lodge under the shadow thereof. The use of the symbol of a tree spreading its branches and giving shelter to those who gather under it is reminiscent of Old Testament passages (Dn 4[12]; Ezek 31[3-6, 12]) and the familiar imagery suggests that Jesus had in view the formation of a community.[13] Other instances are the parables of the Drag-net (Mt 13[47-50]), the Wheat and the Tares (Mt 13[24-30]), and the Vineyard (Mk 12[1-9]). The images which Jesus uses to describe the Kingdom have a corporate significance—the marriage feast, the new temple, and the Shepherd and the flock. 'Fear not, little flock; for it is your Father's good pleasure to give you the kingdom' (Lk 12[32]). This passage takes us back to Micah 5[4]: 'And he shall stand, and shall feed his flock in the strength of the Lord', and to Ezek 34[12-24]). In the passage from Micah, the 'flock' represents those who survive the judgement and is thus an eschatological idea. The 'little flock' are the remnant, the new Israel of God, sent out by their Lord, the great Shepherd of the sheep, to seek and save the lost. For them a new shrine is to be built in which they

[13] cf. R. N. Flew, *Jesus and His Church* (1938), pp. 36-9.

may worship and serve God as His people. 'I will destroy this temple that is made with hands, and in three days I will build another made without hands'[14] (Mk 14:58; Mt 26:60b-61; cf. Jn 2:19).

(iii) The Messianic vocation of Jesus as interpreted by Him in the light of the Servant of God described in the 'Servant Songs' of Second Isaiah and the 'Son of man' in the Book of Daniel carries with it the idea of a community. Whatever may be the view taken of the identity of the Servant, it is clear that He is represented as creating by His sufferings a new community which becomes the organ of God's redemptive purpose in the world. Although the corporate interpretation of the 'Son of man' sayings advanced by Professor Manson creates difficulties, there is sufficient evidence in the Gospels to show that Jesus desired that His disciples should share in His sufferings and triumphs, and become united to Him in His obedience to the divine Rule. As 'Son of man' He was the representative of a new people whom He gathered that they might be the bearers of the divine Rule to men. In the Book of Daniel, as in the teaching of Jesus, the Son of Man has a corporate background.

(iv) Jesus called twelve disciples 'that they might be with him, and that he might send them forth to preach' (Mk 3:14). The appointment of the disciples should be viewed in the light of the group of disciples gathered by Isaiah (Is 8:16-18), which the late Robertson Smith[15] described as the birth of the conception of the Church. The number selected cannot have been accidental, since it is that of the tribes of Israel. He sends them forth as his ambassadors and their message was to be 'The Rule of God has come upon you'[16] (Mk 6:7-13; Mt 9:1-6; Lk 9:1-6, 10:1-20). In His choice of disciples, in His training of them, and in the task which He entrusted to them, Jesus reveals His intention of creating a new community, the new Israel of God committed to the Rule of God.

(v) The Last Supper presupposes a community. The idea of the Covenant embodied in the Last Supper itself and in the words

---

[14] Whatever may have been the original form of the saying, its authenticity is widely accepted and it is most satisfactorily explained as referring to the Messianic judgement on the old Israel and the creation of the New Israel by the Messiah. (cf. R. N. Flew, *Jesus and His Church*, pp. 55f.; Otto, *The Kingdom of God and the Son of Man*, p. 62.)

[15] *Prophets of Israel*, p. 275 (New edn, 1897).

[16] It may be that the mission of the seventy is a doublet of the mission to the twelve although this theory is not necessary.

'This is my blood of the covenant, which is shed for many' (Mk 14^{24f.}) implies the formation of a new community, the redeemed people of God. In the Old Testament, the conception of the Covenant is corporate. The covenant at Sinai constituted disorganized tribes into the people of God and, if the new covenant in Jeremiah moves on a higher spiritual plane with deeper implications for the individual, it is still a covenant with the house of Israel: 'And I will be their God, and they shall be my people' (Jer 31³³). When our Lord spoke the words about the covenant at the Last Supper, the creation of a new community united to Him in obedience to God and the service of man must have been present to His mind.

The Rule of God as interpreted by Jesus implies the Church, the new Israel, the people of God, charged to live under the kingly Rule of God, and commissioned as envoys of the Son of Man to proclaim divine salvation to men in the new age which had dawned.

(6) *The Kingdom of God in the teaching of Jesus involves the Cross*

If the Kingdom was present in Jesus, then He did not die to bring the Kingdom in. He died to manifest the Kingdom that had come with Him and to make it possible for men to avail themselves of its power. The main burden which our Lord had to bear was the hardness of the human heart. He brought to men as the bearer of the divine Rule the free forgiveness of God, but without repentance the gift could not be received. It was in order to open up a way whereby men might turn to God that He went to the Cross. Though we do not know when Jesus first became conscious of the necessity of the Cross, there is reason to believe that from the beginning the idea of suffering was indissolubly woven into His consciousness of vocation as Messiah. The connexion between them is significantly brought out in the narrative of His Baptism, where we have the combination of the ideal king of Israel in the second Psalm with the 'servant' of Second Isaiah (Mk 1⁹⁻¹¹=Lk 3²¹⁻²=Mt 3¹³⁻¹⁷, Ps 2⁷, Is 42¹).

The story of the Temptation does not imply that He envisaged the Cross but it does mean that He knew that complete obedience to the will of God in this world involved self-abnegation and the opposition of friends and foes. Cæsarea Philippi constituted a crisis, and the path of suffering which had been foreseen was more clearly marked out in His mind as He reflected upon the fate of John, the growing opposition of Scribes and Pharisees, and the apparent failure of His mission. The problem that faced Him was not how could God forgive, but how could men be brought to repentance. He knew no other way than that of committing Himself at every stage to God's Rule, so that through His sacrifice of obedience men might end their rebellion and become reconciled to God and His purpose for their lives. The Cross is thus not a condition of the coming of the Kingdom but the Kingdom itself coming with power.

CHAPTER TWO

THE DOCTRINE OF GOD

(1) SOVEREIGN LOVE

WE are now in a position to consider the theological implications of the teaching of Jesus about the Kingdom of God, and the beginning and the end of our quest is the doctrine of God. The teaching of Jesus presupposes that God is Sovereign Love. What are we to understand by the conception of God as Sovereign Love?

(1) First, when we speak of God as Sovereign Love we mean that He is personal. To ascribe personality to God is to conceive of Him as a self-conscious being, active will, living, creative, responsive to human need, transcending the universe in His unique individuality yet universally present within it, and governed in all His activities by an unchanging purpose. For the biblical writers, what we in abstract language describe as the personality of God meant pre-eminently the living God. 'The Lord,' says Jeremiah, 'is the living God, and an everlasting king' (10^{10}). He is further known to be a living God, in the light of the witness of the Bible, by His marvellous works.

There are many philosophical problems raised by the idea of God as personal which lie beyond the limits of the present study. The reservations which some experience in speaking about God as personal, however, do not arise from any particular interest in the abstruse questions raised by personality, human or divine. They may be traced to three sources. First, the immensity of the universe as revealed by modern science, the dominance of modern science itself which is preoccupied with the type rather than the individual, and the growing complexity of the pattern of modern life suggest that the ultimate nature of life is impersonal. Secondly, we all tend to regard ourselves as somehow apart from the universe, and we forget that we as beings who think and know and act are parts of the problem which we are seeking to solve. This tendency to isolate ourselves from our environment is common enough in many spheres. There are members of the Christian Church who pass judgement on the Church as though they themselves had no part or place in it, and a Government which has been elected by democratic vote is viewed by the electors as an alien body whose policy has no connexion with their desires. But if we are to understand the final nature of things, it is necessary to take into account personal life, which is by common consent the highest product of the universe, and it may be that in personality we shall find the key to the enigma. Thirdly, it is frequently urged that to attribute personality to God is to lay ourselves open to the charge of anthropomorphism.

Obviously all our thinking is anthropomorphic whether it be related to science or theology, but probably what is meant by this vaguely expressed objection is that we cannot apply to God the limitations of human personality. With that contention nobody presumably would wish to disagree. Human personality develops through fellowship, and the self, which is related to its states but cannot be identified with them, does not achieve the status of personality until some degree of unity arising from the pursuit of an ideal has been achieved. There are areas of our life which have not yet been brought under the control of those ideals to which supreme worth is attached, and for that reason we lack the integration which is the hall-mark of mature personality. If, indeed, human personality exhausted the meaning of personality, we should have to consider whether, in spite of the fact that it is the highest reach of human experience, we could appropriately conceive of God as personal. To affirm personality in God, however, does not mean that for Him personality is an achievement gained as the result of conflict and strife, and made possible by the growth of a social and ethical consciousness. Nor can it be maintained that, since in human experience personality is conditioned by progress in thought and moral insight and knowledge of other selves, development is of its essence. We cannot, it is true, ascribe self-consciousness to God in any satisfactory sense unless within the divine unity there are distinctions, and it may be said that it is the denial of the reality of the distinctions expressed in the doctrine of the Trinity that reduces the conception of God to an abstraction.

While, then, we need to dissociate personality in God from some of the embodiments of personality in man, we may speak of God as personal in a sense which is not fundamentally different from that in which we employ the term in reference to ourselves. To avoid the baser kind of anthropomorphism, it is sometimes suggested that the term 'supra-personal' should be used. Although there is no serious objection to this term, it should be recognized that its adoption may foster the conception of God as impersonal and obscure the reality of the personal encounter between God and man in worship, thought, and daily life.

(2) Secondly, the conception of God as Sovereign Love implies that He is other than we are. In theological writings, the interpretation of the nature of God by reference to His attributes has sometimes concealed His essential unity and created such seeming contradictions as that between His love and His righteousness. And yet while the attributes of God must be held together in an indissoluble unity, it is sometimes conducive to clarity to examine them singly as distinctive aspects of divine Personality. Here we shall confine ourselves to the consideration of the nature of God as creative and eternal, and as love. These three attributes set out in bold relief the fundamental difference between God and man.

(i) The Christian doctrine of God as Creator is concerned to say one thing: man and the world are dependent upon God. The relation of man to God is not that of equality but of dependence. The world and ourselves are the creation of His active will. This view of the relation of God to the world is to be distinguished from pantheism which implies that God and the universe are one, and men as well as things are modes of His being. Plainly pantheism in its varied forms can find no room for human freedom or for the distinction between right and wrong. If nothing but God exists, man ceases to be personal and communion with God means absorption in deity. Further, if the theory is to be strictly maintained, it means that Nero is as much a part of God as St Paul.

Again, we have to distinguish the Christian doctrine of creation from the notion that the world has somehow emanated from God as though God by an inner necessity unfolded Himself into the world of men and things. How God as a Spiritual Being can unfold Himself into material objects in space is difficult to understand. This view encounters all the objections that may be raised against pantheism. Then the Christian idea of creation is opposed to the belief that God created the world out of material already in existence. Apart from the fact that this conception, sometimes described as dualism, is based entirely upon our own creative activity, where material is ready to hand, it has no explanation to offer of the origin of the matter which God is alleged to have used in His creative work.

To say that God created the world out of nothing may not be particularly illuminating, although it sometimes receives confirmation from unlikely quarters. 'From time to time,' writes Fred Hoyle in advancing the theory of continuous creation, 'people ask where the created world comes from. Well, it does not come from anywhere. Material simply appears—it is created.'[1] The idea of creation out of nothing is not, however, intended to form the basis of a dogmatic pronouncement. No such pronouncement is possible in the present or, we may venture to predict, in the future state of our knowledge. The creative activity of man may shed some light on the creative activity of God. We may think of the poet or painter who gives expression to the vision that surges within him and which seems to take charge of his mind. But the artist is dependent on material which he has not created, before he can fully reveal to himself or to others the content of his thought and emotions. The creative activity of God is unique and lies beyond our comprehension. At every stage of the creative process which is continuous, the world and ourselves are dependent upon God. Discussions relating to the question whether creation had a beginning in time or 'with time' do not affect the essential significance of the idea of creation.

If the doctrine of creation is interpreted as the dependence of the world upon God, some of the difficulties which otherwise seem to invalidate it do not arise. The notion that God for many ages remained inactive and then at a comparatively late date created the world presents insuperable objections. This view presupposes that eternity preceded time and that God is not eternally creative. Here, in the picture of God first contemplating the idea of a universe and then resolving to bring it into existence, we have a clear instance of the contradictions in which we are involved when we fail to recognize the limitations of human

[1] *The Nature of the Universe* (1950), p. 105.

analogies. We cannot conceive of God apart from a created order, although this does not mean that the physical universe or any other system is eternal, nor does it carry with it the implication that God is dependent in an absolute sense upon the creation. What it does affirm is that God who is personal is creative, and that God considered wholly apart from His creative activity and from created being ceases to be personal. Christian theologians have been rightly anxious to safeguard the otherness of God. Hence in opposition to Gnostic, Manichæan, and other forms of dualism, Neo-Platonic emanations and pantheistic systems, they have spoken of 'creation out of nothing', which is another way of saying that God is not governed by any limitations external to Himself. Their insistence on a beginning in time has been at least partly stimulated by the same motive, since it appeared that the repudiation of the idea of an absolute beginning would involve the acceptance of the belief in the eternity of the universe, and dualism would therefore once again have reasserted itself. Christian theology has been concerned to affirm the doctrine that the universe finds its explanation in One who is not to be identified with it but who cannot be conceived by us out of relation to it. God is other than the creation and He is other than finite beings. He is dependent upon created being only in the sense that it is of His nature to create. Created being is dependent upon God in the sense that God is the source and ground of its existence. Creation, that is, including man, is absolutely dependent upon God.

(ii) The otherness of God is again brought home to us when we reflect upon God as eternal. 'Eternity' is used in a number of senses. Sometimes it is taken to mean unendingness—time indefinitely extended at both ends. For God, time on this view has neither beginning nor end, although we are not told what kind of time it is that has no conclusion. Unendingness as such has no religious significance. But there lies behind what appears to be a somewhat crude quantitative conception the belief that 'time which like an ever-rolling stream bears all its sons away' does not take its toll of God. Eternity again is sometimes interpreted as timelessness. 'Yesterday', 'today', tomorrow', have no place in the divine experience. If for the divine experience the time-process is unreal, it is difficult to see how God can be the ground of creation, which is under the form of time, and how, if He is wholly outside time, He could make Himself known to man. Then eternity has been given the meaning of simultaneity. That is, God sees things all together. Past, present and future are merged into a perfect unity, or what is described as one 'eternal now', just as in a flash of insight we may see the significance of a whole series of events. It is claimed that the literature of mysticism affords illustrations of a kindred experience in which the mystic rises above successiveness and blends all things in one single act of apprehension. Baron von Hügel, in expounding this idea with reference to mystical experience,[2] quotes St Augustine's words: In the next life 'perhaps our own thoughts also will not be flowing, going from one thing to another, but we shall see all we know simultaneously in one intuition'. This sense of 'eternity', if pressed, apart from the difficulty raised by inclusion of the future, results in a view which excludes from the divine experience the discrimination of past, present, and future. Hence, once again, the time-process is regarded as ultimately unreal, even if we are reminded by the submission that succession has no meaning for God, that He is not controlled by the changes and chances of this fleeting life.

In what direction are we to look for a more satisfactory concept of 'eternity'? Our own experience may provide a clue. We are conscious of change, or succession. Time—past, present, future— is the form of our experience. And yet we are not simply children of time. We are aware of ourselves as persisting through the succession of changes which we experience. It is the fact that we stand above time, although we are within it, that enables us to attain the status of persons. We are able to review the past and envisage the future. Events are determined to some degree by our volition. We are creatures of time but we transcend it. The conceptions of transcendence and immanence may thus be applied to man in his relation to time.

The Christian understanding of the doctrine of God as eternal is that He pursues an immutable purpose in this world of change. Our relation to time is beset by many limitations. Memory often plays us false and there is much that even the most retentive mind cannot recall. Even when events are recalled, they may be erroneously interpreted. Plans for the immediate or remote

[2] *The Mystical Element of Religion* (1908), II.248.

future may be rendered null and void owing to unexpected developments. And how fickle is our pursuit of a purpose which has commended itself to our mind and conscience! God is other than we are. His span of time covers all events, and by reason of His complete knowledge He is able to see history in its totality. We are not, however, to conclude that past, present and future have no meaning for God and that He dwells above the time-process. 'Then', 'now', 'not yet', are significant in the divine experience. The Kingdom of God, as we have seen, is past, present, and future, and this distinction holds surely for God as for ourselves. While God accomplishes His purpose through the events of history, His activity is determined by His unchanging nature. He is in complete control of the world which He has created and is directing events toward the fulfilment of His immutable will which is perfect love.

(iii) The otherness of God is made unmistakably plain when we come to the distinctively Christian conception of the Love of God. With that conception we shall be more fully concerned in the next section, where it will become evident that there is no conflict between the righteousness of God and His love. Those who set these qualities in opposition to each other fail either to interpret aright the meaning of righteousness or of love. There is no righteousness apart from love and there is no love that does not conform to righteousness. He is a 'righteous God and a Saviour',[3] and, we may add, a Saviour and a righteous God. What we are specially concerned to note here is that the quality of divine love stands in marked contrast to the quality of human love. Though the distinction between *agape* and *eros* in the well-known work of Nygren[4] is doubtless pressed too far, it is of fundamental importance. It will be recalled that Nygren contends that while the conception of *agape* is the child of Christianity, the *eros*-motif is the product of Hellenism as found in Aristotle but pre-eminently in Plato. In Christian theology, we are told, *agape* and *eros*, which are distinct conceptions, have been confused, and the fundamental character of the Christian Gospel has thus been obscured. *Agape* is God's unconditioned love, universal and free, but *eros* is determined by man's sense of need or of some defect.

[3] cf. N. H. Snaith, *The Distinctive Ideas of the Old Testament* (1944), esp. Chs 3 and 4.
[4] *Agape and Eros* (E.T., 1953, P. S. Watson).

We love because a person by reason of his obvious worth or enduring qualities or kindred interests calls forth our love. That is, the person satisfies some desire in us or enriches our experience. Our approach to God even at the higher levels of religious experience is determined by a sense of need which God alone can supply. Even our praise is inspired by Him. God, on the other hand, does not love a man on the ground of merit, or in order to fill up what is lacking in His own experience. *Agape*, Nygren affirms, is the direct opposite of that love which is called out by the worthiness of its object, since man's value consists simply in the fact that God loves him. The love of God is always prior to our love of God, although His Love, *agape*, may be put into us and we may manifest it in our dealings with others. Nygren, it is true, is in danger of speaking of man as a created object in whom there is nothing worthy of love: 'The man whom God loves,' we are told, 'has no value in himself. What gives him value is precisely the fact that God loves him.'[5] But he has value in himself, because He is the child of God who created Him, and although his nature has been corrupted by sin, he is still the child of God and thus the object of divine love. Nevertheless, Nygren has rendered much-needed service in reminding us of the fundamental difference between human and divine love. Since man has been made in the image of God, and this has not been obliterated in spite of his many betrayals, there are traces of divine love in his personal relations, particularly in parental love. And when the redeeming power of the love of God has been given freedom to penetrate the deeps of our personality, we learn to love our enemies and those to whom we are not drawn by natural desire or inclination, because in creation and redemption God has set his love upon them and His love dwells in us.

God, then, is other than we are. The recognition of the otherness of God is an antidote to superficial thinking and acts as a safeguard against a spurious simplicity in our conception of God. The plea for intelligibility in religion may easily become a cloak for shallowness. By all means let our theology be lucid, and let it be set forth in relation to contemporary thought. No Christian, without betraying his heritage, can have any part in the flight from reason, nor can he set a premium upon a religious experience that ignores intellectual demands. Pusey may have displayed

[5] op. cit., p. 78.

little understanding of historic Methodism when he said that in Methodism salvation by faith meant salvation by feeling, but it must be admitted that some of the earlier and later followers of Wesley provided him with some excuse for this misrepresentation. God, however, cannot be contained in the thought-forms of any age and while the element of mystery must not be used as a convenient way of escape for theologians who are harassed by the latest challenge of historical criticism, philosophy, or science, the final truth about God defies complete expression in intellectual terms.

Further, the conviction of the otherness of God keeps our faith firm in the face of prevailing unbelief and the vagaries of our own religious experience. The reality of God is not dependent upon the consent of contemporary theories or upon changing moods. The acceptance or rejection of His Rule does not affect its validity, since it is the rule of the unchanging God, the Creator of the world and its sovereign Lord. Again the recollection of the otherness of God enriches our worship and gives to it a majestic and spacious content. It is a buttress against what Professor Farmer has called being 'pally with deity'. Worship is an offering to one who is other than we are, not only in the sense that He exists independently of us and is the source of our ideals, but in the sense that our noblest thoughts are only a pale reflexion of His mercy, truth, and love. If this thought is allowed to permeate our worship, adoration will become spontaneous, and what may appear to be a disabling tension between God and man will open up a way to a life of perfect communion.

(3) The conception of God as Sovereign Love implies the activity of God in history. God is active will; the living God and the Rule of God comes with power because it is God Himself in action. The sphere of the divine activity is history, and we may well ask: 'What is history?' Is it simply a succession of events devoid of meaning or unity? Is it the scene of the progressive realization of an ideal? Is it to some degree unreal? Plato and the Stoics found history something of an encumbrance. Particular things and particular events were for them in some sense unreal, since what is real is one and unchanging. The Stoics believed that the real is the rational, although the rational cannot be given in individual and sensible things. They and Plato tried to find room for the series of historic events by having recourse to the

cyclic theory—that there is nothing new under the sun and what has happened will happen again. There is, it was thought, a law of recurrence which is constant, and their belief in the unchanging nature of the real was thus preserved.

According to the biblical view, history is not a succession or cycle of events, but processes ripening into a crisis or opportunity. The significant biblical term is not time in the sense of duration; it is time as opportunity or fulfilment. Hence the Bible is concerned not so much with *chronos* (measured time) as with *kairos*, which means time as opportunity. It is God who provides the opportunity, and who charges the events with their content so that they may serve as a challenge and evoke a response. In every crisis—the deliverance from Egypt, the exile, the Return, the life, death, and resurrection of Christ—God presents an opportunity, and subsequent history is determined by the decision which is taken by man. God is active throughout in revelation and redemption.

The recovery of the concept of revelation is among the most important features of theological thought during the past thirty years. It is significant that the increasing emphasis upon this concept among theologians is found alongside a growing aversion in some schools of modern philosophy to take it into account. Such schools have abandoned the traditional function of philosophy, which was held to be the interpretation of the universe when viewed as a whole. Some of the questions discussed, for example, by the late G. F. Stout in his recently published second volume of Gifford Lectures, delivered in 1919 and 1921, seem singularly remote in the light of contemporary philosophical tendencies. The repudiation of mechanical or dialectical materialism or different forms of monism does not mean that the climate is more favourable to the consideration of the conceptions of revelation, the Incarnation and the Atonement. If we assume that the world has no meaning, or that if it has a meaning we cannot discover it because of the necessary limitations of scientific knowledge, no useful purpose is served by exploring the content of what is alleged to be divine revelation. On the other hand, if knowledge is not confined to what can be verified by scientific method or by reference to sense experience alone, it may be that the content of divine revelation will provide the solution of the enigma of human life.

Let us therefore look at the content of the revelation of God recorded in the Bible. Revelation in the Scriptures is given, not in a series of propositions or ideas, but in persons and events. The view that it is given in the former way is due largely to the dominance of Greek thought in the Church, and although there is an obligation resting upon us to recollect what Christianity owes to the Greek as well as to the Hebrew, we must recognize that the Bible is concerned primarily not with ideas, but with events. It is a history book, which singles out certain events as supremely expressive of the nature and purpose of God.

The biblical story is bound up with the institution of the covenant. God elects a particular people and binds Himself to them. He is represented as guiding and moulding their history so that they may become the agents of His righteous rule among the nations. They prove faithless and turn their back on the divine task entrusted to them. Consumed by nationalistic ambitions, their exclusiveness becomes the cause of their fall. A remnant, however, remains, which looks to the day when Israel shall be the third with Egypt and Syria, a blessing in the midst of the earth. The Remnant dwindles, and it may be that in Deutero-Isaiah, in the figure of the Servant, we have an individual who represents the age-long purpose of God for Israel.

When we turn to the New Testament, revelation is still given, as alone it can be given, through history. The true Israel of God is unveiled in the person and work of the Messiah, and as Son of Man Jesus re-creates and reconstitutes the Old Israel, so that it may become the instrument and expression of the Kingly Rule of God present in Him. With Him, the Kingdom of God, the end to which history is moving, is in action, and the New Testament confidently anticipates the final coming of the Kingdom of God by the power of God Himself in a transformed universe. The ground of its hope is the conviction that in Christ God has spoken once and for all, and made known His eternal purpose.

The conception of revelation underlying the biblical record presents certain problems to the contemporary mind. Where there is a disposition to accept the theistic view, which regards the universe as the expression of the purpose of a personal Being who unites in Himself power and love, there appears to be no insuperable difficulty in countenancing the idea of general revelation. If God is creative love, the absence of revelation in some form would require explanation, since it is of the nature of love to reveal itself. Hence theism presupposes the disclosure of God in creation and in man, in the insight of poets and prophets, and in the achievements of science and art. What is challenged is the affirmation that in one particular person, who lived in a particular country at a particular time, God uniquely revealed Himself, and that the revelation was universal and final.

First, let it be said that Christianity does not claim that a complete revelation of God has been given in the person and work of Jesus Christ. What it declares is that God has unveiled His eternal purpose in Him, and that by so doing He has revealed His own nature. The character or nature of God can only be made known in personal life. It is in concrete and particular acts or events that character is disclosed. The last act of Captain Scott's life showed the quality of his character as nothing else could, and if we are concerned to know what kind of a man he was we have the answer in that deed of self-renunciation. A considerable part of our life is spent in routine activities—sleep, food, work, recreation—and they may not disclose anything distinctive about us. But a crisis such as a personal disappointment or sorrow in our own life arises, and our true nature is unveiled.

The same principle may be illustrated from the sphere of art. It is not from books about pictures that we come to an authentic appreciation of beauty, although they may help us to look for the right things in works of art. We must stand before the pictures themselves and allow them to communicate their secret to us. A picture has particularity. The artist conveys his vision to the canvas. He concentrates attention upon an isolated scene and seeks to express what he sees. What is not considered essential for a true expression of that which has been impressed upon his mind he prunes away, for puritanism is of the essence of art as of moral character. The picture is set in a frame, not because the frame has intrinsic value, but in order that our attention may be more easily focused on the picture. What the artist conveys at a particular time with a particular brush and canvas has a universal meaning. A great picture, once you have perceived what the artist meant you to perceive, lives with you always. It may bear a date, but the beauty it enshrines is an eternal possession.

THE DOCTRINE OF GOD

Let us now look again at the idea of divine revelation. The revelation of God, given through unique situations and persons woven into the fabric of the divine purpose by God Himself, reached its fulfilment in Jesus Christ, in whom, according to the teaching of the New Testament as interpreted by the Christian Church, God Himself was personally present. Within the framework of human experience God manifested His sovereign love. The limits of time and space did not distort the revelation. They made it possible for God to make Himself known. The truth about His nature and Rule had to be set in a bodily frame in order that it might be discerned. There are aspects of the divine Being which are hidden from finite minds. God outside human experience we cannot hope to know. God in human experience comes within the range of our apprehension.

If in Christ we have a revelation of the character and purpose of God, we may justly speak of it as a revelation given once and for all. There is much about God which Jesus left unsaid, but He left us in no doubt as to His character and His eternal purpose. If Jesus had appeared today rather than two thousand years ago, the content of the revelation would be unaltered, although there would be a change of setting, thought-forms and language. The revelation concerns God and His Rule, which are immutable. We are still under the control of the theory of inevitable progress, and we imagine that 'today' must of necessity be advance on 'yesterday', and that the later in time invariably supersedes the earlier. In science the later theory is generally an advance upon the earlier. If medical or surgical treatment becomes necessary we prefer, for the most part, to avail ourselves of the resources of the latest discoveries rather than to fall back on ancient methods of healing. Further, there have been what most of us would account great steps of human progress in the abolition of slavery over the larger part of the earth, the increase of educational facilities, the betterment of industrial conditions and the growing concern for the welfare of the young and the aged. In the ordering of human life, the later often marks an advance upon the earlier. Nevertheless, there are spheres in which the later does not supersede the earlier, and in which achievements are not affected by the passage of time. The sculpture of the age of Pericles is not likely to be superseded, nor is it probable that a greater than Homer or Shakespeare will arise. Indeed it would appear that in art and literature the peak may be reached at a comparatively early stage. A work of art may be perfect in its own order irrespective of its date. Even if at a later time other works are produced which can also be so described, they will not supplant or in any way affect the merit of earlier works.

Turn again to the question of character. Nobody would claim that a son must be a better man than his father because he came after him and had perhaps superior advantages. Fathers and perhaps sons would certainly rebut the assumption of inevitable progress in family history. When we compare ourselves with some of the men and women of former ages, within and without the Christian Church, we are more conscious of the poverty of our moral and spiritual achievements than of the gulf in time that divides us. It is significant that most of the classics of religious devotion belong to the distant past, and that there are certain gifts such as that of composing liturgies, which, judging from some contemporary effusions, seem to have been irretrievably lost.

In view of these elementary considerations, there seems to be no insuperable objection to the view that the supreme revelation of the character of God was given at a comparatively early stage in human history. That the final revelation should have come early, or that it should be 'once and for all' if it is a revelation of the character of the eternal God, is not destructive of progress. It is indeed the precondition of progress. The Rule of God which came with Jesus is the Rule of love, and love is creative. It seeks to become incarnate in every fresh situation, and to discover new objects which can be brought within its power. Finality may be creative or static. There was a finality about the Jewish Law which led to the closing of the mind and to the inability to recognize new truth when it was presented. If there are Christian communions today which are critical of the emphasis on the structure of the Church and insist on a clear distinction being made between faith and order, it should be remembered that, with the history of the Church in mind, they recall how easily even Christians may substitute legalism for grace and a static for a creative finality. The Rule of Grace can only have meaning in a world of persons and while, as we have seen, growth and development are not to be ascribed to the personal life of God, they are inseparable from the personal life of man. The acceptance of the

Rule of Grace active and present in Jesus is not the end of the Christian journey, but the beginning. Those who pledge their allegiance to it are led into situations for which there are no parallels in the Gospel, and it is therefore impossible to produce a complete code of Christian behaviour. There is a sense in which it is true to say that Christian ethics as a science of conduct does not exist. We may speak of a Christian way of life which is the expression of fellowship between man and God as revealed in Christ, but the Christian way cannot be converted into an ethical system without misrepresenting its character as a living creative personal relationship. The finality of the Christian Faith lies in the revelation of the end to which history is moving—the Kingdom of God, manifest in the life, death, and resurrection of Christ and dynamically at work in human life. It is the revelation of the end that gives security to the Christian adventure. Before we can make a fruitful advance in any sphere, we need to know where we are going. The direction must be fixed. Hence the finality of the Christian revelation means, not that progress has reached its zenith, but that the goal of progress has been unambiguously disclosed. The way is now open to work out the significance of what has been given, once and for all, in worship, thought and conduct, in the life of the individual and in the wider life of the community. In that enterprise those who share varying traditions and who belong to different races and nations have their part to play. If East and West were to respond to the revelation of God in Christ and live by its light and power, they would be free to explore the inexhaustible treasures of a common Faith. There are aspects of the Christian Revelation which no one nation or religious tradition can express. When the differing interpretations of the one revelation are held together, we shall have a fullness of understanding in which all may share.

To sum up, revelation is a divine act; it is something which God does. And what He does is to unveil His eternal nature and purpose through the events of history. Christianity affirms that Christ, in whom the divine Rule was actively present, is the final revelation of the ways of God. He has done something which does not need to be done again. Whether or not men repent, God has spoken His final word about His relation to mankind. But how is man to be reconciled to it? How is he to turn to God and recognize the truth unveiled? The end of revelation is redemption. Revelation and redemption are inseparable elements in one process. God reveals Himself, not in order that He may demonstrate His power, but in order that He may reconcile men to His kingly Rule.

(II) REDEMPTION

The redemptive activity of God is centred in the Cross of Christ. It did not begin with the Cross, but found its fulfilment there. We have already referred to the teaching of Jesus about the Kingdom in relation to the Cross, and its implications must now be considered.

First, the Cross is God's Kingly Rule in action. It is the Kingdom of God coming with power. Jesus went to the Cross in obedience to the Rule of God and in that act of obedience unveiled the nature of the Kingdom which inspired it.

That Jesus believed the Cross was in accordance with the will of God is abundantly supported by our sources. 'And he began to teach them that the Son of man must suffer many things . . .' (Mk 8^{31}, 9^{31}, 10^{33}). The word 'must' is significant, and the reference is not to external necessity, but to an inward constraint born of a conviction that the way of the Cross was God's way for the Son of man. He speaks of the passion as a cup which comes from the Father's hand (Mk 14^{36}; cf. 10^{38}), and 'cup' in the Old Testament has as its characteristic meaning, suffering appointed by God. The reference is not to physical suffering or death alone, but to the mental agony which arose from an acute consciousness of the reaction of divine love to sin and which culminated in death. Again, He speaks of His passion as a baptism: 'I have a baptism to be baptized with; and how am I straitened till it be accomplished' (Lk 12^{50}). Dr Vincent Taylor[5] observes that there is good reason to believe that in popular Greek '*baptizesthai*' was used metaphorically in the sense of being flooded with calamities, and this judgement is supported by Moulton and Milligan,[6] whom he quotes. Similarly in the Old Testament, in such passages as Psalm 42^7 and Isaiah 43^2, we have the same meaning.[7]

The necessity of the Cross in the thought of Jesus is related to

---

[5] *Jesus and His Sacrifice*, p. 98.   [6] *Vocabulary of the Greek Testament*, p. 102.
[7] cf. W. F. Flemington, *The New Testament Doctrine of Baptism* (1948), pp. 31-2.

His consciousness of his Messianic function. There is no evidence to support the view that Jesus went to His death in order to force the issue and bring in the Kingdom. He died so that men might become reconciled to the Kingdom which had already come but which was to be uniquely manifested in the final act of His earthly life—'The Son of man came not to be ministered unto, but to minister, and to give his life a ransom for many' (Mk 10^{45}). The word 'ransom' need not be pressed unduly, although the meaning of the term, which is that something is done for another to secure his freedom, cannot be disregarded. That the saying stands apart in the recorded sayings of Jesus is no ground for dismissing its authority, unless it could be proved that it was out of harmony with the rest of His teaching. In this passage Jesus is not simply speaking of the purpose of His coming as service to humanity. The service which He renders is fulfilled in an act which brings with it emancipation for man, and there cannot be any serious doubt that it is the power of evil from which man is to be set free. It is probable that the word '*anti*' should be translated 'instead of', and, while a substitutionary meaning must be included, we are not justified in going beyond the idea of representative suffering found in Isaiah 53 in the light of which this passage should be interpreted. But the words 'a ransom for many' do imply that Jesus accomplished something which was beyond the power of man to do for himself, and that what He accomplished was the fulfilment of His Messianic function as Son of Man, the agent of God's Kingly Rule. In so giving His life He was obedient to His divinely appointed task, and was acting under a sense of inward necessity which was the outcome of His union with the will of God.

It is significant that when Jesus speaks of His suffering the title employed for Himself is 'Son of man' (Mk 8^{31}, 14$^{21, 41}$). The necessary relation between the Kingdom and His death is thus unmistakable in His thought. That He believed His death to be the indispensable condition of the establishment of the Kingdom in the hearts of men is indicated by the reference in the sayings of the Last Supper to the Messianic banquet (Mk 14^{25}; Mt 26^{29}; Lk 22^{18})—'I will no more drink of the fruit of the vine, until that day when I drink it new in the kingdom of God'. Jesus here looks beyond His death, and the disciples may be forgiven if the wine meant for them His approaching death and nothing else. We must not infer, however, that these words can be taken to mean that Jesus excludes the thought of His death from the anticipation of the Messianic banquet. On the contrary, His death is necessary for the consummation of the Kingdom. It is because of His redemptive suffering in obedience to the divine will that He is able to look with confidence to the full realization of the Rule of God.

Throughout what has been said about the relation of the Cross to the will of God, we need to bear in mind three ruling considerations. (i) The necessity of the Cross is not to be dissociated from the historical circumstances in which it took place. The Cross was conditioned by historical circumstances, although it was determined by the divine will. (ii) The will of God was not regarded by Jesus as alien or opposed to His own will. He was conscious of perfect unity with God, and nowhere is that unity more perfectly expressed than in the prayer 'Abba, Father, all things are possible unto thee; remove this cup from me: howbeit not what I will, but what thou wilt' (Mk 14[36]). There we have perfect confidence in the will of God far removed from anything that can be described as stoical acquiescence. (iii) The conviction that the Cross was in accordance with the divine will suggests active participation in the redemptive purpose of God rather than passive resignation. Jesus is thereby committed to action. He has a baptism to be baptized with. He comes to serve and to give His life as ransom for many. When the end is at hand, he declares that his accusers will see the Son of Man sitting at the right hand of power and coming with the clouds of heaven (Mk 14[62]). He waged unceasing warfare with the powers of evil, and the Cross was the culmination of his unwavering obedience to the kingly rule of God.

Secondly, the Cross reveals the judgement of God. The conception of God as Judge is deeply embedded in the Old and New Testament. God is conceived as King and Judge, and His judgement lies in the active manifestation of His righteousness upon which the world has been firmly fixed. He is eternally Judge of men and nations, since He is eternally righteous and eternally King. His judgement, however, has a present and future reference. In every crisis His righteousness is made known and at the end of history it will be finally unveiled. Hence in the Old Testament, history is to be consummated in the 'Day of the Lord'

THE DOCTRINE OF GOD

which will be a Day of Judgement, and in the New in the final coming of Christ.

We are here concerned with the relation of the Judgement of God to the Cross which has loomed large in the history of the doctrine of the Atonement. If the judgement of God is active in crises—and 'crisis' is Greek for judgement—in what sense is the Cross to be described as the divine judgement? The reaction against the idea of the Cross as the judgement of God among those who do not take a light view of sin is due to some of its debased associations which cannot be harmonized with the Christian revelation. Forgiveness has sometimes been made conditional upon the punishment of sin, and the righteousness of God has been severed from His love. Thus penal views of the Atonement have arisen which seem to suggest an ethical level transcended by man himself. If, however, we ignore the idea of divine judgement, we shall not only fail to represent an essential element in the teaching of Jesus and the Bible as a whole, but shall empty the Gospel of its redemptive significance, since judgement is inseparable from redemption.

The kingly rule of God is the rule of love, and love, as we have seen, is inseparable from righteousness. God's dealings with us are controlled by His purpose to bring us into fellowship with Himself as free and responsible beings, and He is thus unutterably opposed to everything in our life which frustrates that end. Sin, which is rebellion against God, sets in motion a train of inescapable consequences which are grounded in the nature of the universe as the creation of God. Because God is God, He must repudiate sin. And there is only one way in which sin can be repudiated by God, and that is by revealing its true character in its consequences. Judgement is, then, the revelation of the truth of the righteous purpose of God, who is love, in its relation to the consequences of sin. There is nothing arbitrary about its operation and, far from being contradictory of the love of God, judgement is an expression of its redeeming power. If the supreme blessing of the kingly rule is communion with God, which implies the forgiveness of sins, sin must be recognized as enmity against God. One reason why many today are not conscious of the need for forgiveness is that, veiled in self-deception, they do not recognize the reality of sin as rebellion, conscious or unconscious, against God. Unless we recognize that there is something in us that needs forgiveness, obviously forgiveness will not be sought. Judgement, as the revelation of the nature of our condition and of the consequences of our broken sonship, is the handmaid of mercy. It is the precondition of fellowship with God.

The Cross represents the evil consequences of the sin of the world—dishonest and crooked thinking, moral obtuseness, pride, the closed mind, irresponsibility of rulers, ingratitude, treachery, disloyalty. The solidarity of evil was confronted by the perfect obedience of Christ to the Rule of God, and in that encounter evil was revealed for what it is. Against the background of our shuffling and compromise, our fitful obedience to the will of God, and our concern for our own interests, even though we profess to have entered into the Kingdom of God, the sin of the world fails to stand out in its true nature. Seen against the background of perfect obedience in which the love of God is completely manifested, it constitutes its own condemnation.

Divine judgement, however, is a personal attribute of the redeeming God; it is God Himself in action. In order to avoid the danger of harbouring unethical and irrational conceptions of divine judgement, there has been a growing tendency to speak of the inevitable consequences of sin rather than of divine judgement. There are three objections to the exclusive identification of judgement with the consequences of Sin. (i) It depersonalizes our relationship to God and thus obscures the fact that sin is primarily alienation from God. (ii) It fails to recognize that God Himself is active within the situation which sin has created, bringing home to the mind and conscience the need for forgiveness. Sin means alienation—not separation from God. The identification of the consequences of sin with the law of cause and effect seems to give to the principle of retribution a status relatively independent of God and His redeeming work. (iii) Judgement is love in action. While man identifies himself with sin God is opposed to him. His wrath, which is the fire of love, destined to consume everything that is contrary to itself, is made manifest. But the purpose of the wrath of God, which is inseparable from His love, is not to destroy but to redeem.

The Cross is the judgement of God upon sin, not because Christ on the Cross is our penal substitute or because He suffers the final punishment of sin, but because it reveals to those whose eyes have been opened the nature of sin, and thus prepares the way for the awakening of the consciousness of the need for forgiveness. To that end, Jesus drank the cup of suffering, and so identified himself with sinful man as to experience the utter desolation and isolation from God to which sin leads (Mk 14^{34}, 15^{34}). He thus bears in His own body and mind the consequences of the sin of the world, and in those consequences there is revealed the judgement of God—the divine verdict on sin.

Thirdly, the Cross brings reconciliation to God's Kingly Rule, or peace with God. To be reconciled, or to accept God's Kingly Rule, first of all means forgiveness, and forgiveness in the Synoptic Gospels can mean nothing less than restoration to God's family, if the true setting of the teaching of Jesus is the Kingdom of God. To be forgiven involves something more than the cancellation of the past. It implies that the power of the past has been broken even though its consequences live on. When a man is set in a new relationship to God, the past no longer represents him. Our representative is Christ crucified. Hence, and this is the second meaning of reconciliation, we are gathered into the new humanity, the new covenant in His blood, and the fruits of reconciliation are revealed in peace with God and obedience to His rule over the whole area of our life. Reconciliation is made possible by the life of obedience to the will of God being put into us so that we are made all over again.

The Cross is thus a representative sacrifice, offered so that man may be reconciled to God. It is offered to God on behalf of men. And when we speak of the death of Christ as a sacrifice, we mean that personal and moral act of personal dedication to the will of God which issued in the Cross. At every stage of the conflict with the powers of evil, He made a sacrifice of total obedience, and His death completed what His life began. Perhaps the most significant passage in this connexion is found in Mk 14^{24}: 'This is my blood of the covenant, which is shed for many' (1 Cor 11^{25}: 'This cup is the new covenant in my blood'). The new covenant, like the old, implies that God has taken the initiative and that He has made it possible for man to enter into a new relationship with Himself. The covenant denotes a new order of personal relations. The background of the saying may have been Exodus 24^8 where we read of the ratifying of the covenant by the sprinkling of the sacrificial blood, or the covenant promised by Jeremiah (31$^{31-4}$), or the references to the covenant in the Servant Songs (Is 42⁶, 49⁸)—'I will ... give thee for a covenant of the people'. It may be that instead of seeking the background of our Lord's thought at the Supper in this passage rather than that, we should see it in a combination of Jeremiah's new covenant and in the vocation of Himself as Servant. By His blood, or by offering His life for others, He establishes a new order or covenant of grace into which men may enter. It is the order of God's Kingly Rule.

The final meaning of the Cross is fellowship with the Sufferings of Christ. St Paul, in his conception of faith-union with Christ, brings out this thought with greater fullness than the writers of the Synoptic Gospels, but his teaching represents a conviction which goes back to the Mind of Jesus. Christ's suffering was representative, not only in the sense that He acted on behalf of humanity, but in the sense that man may share in His act of obedience to God's Kingly Rule and thus in its redemptive activity. It is as Son of Man that He goes as it is written of Him, and as He goes He would take others with Him. They are to take up the Cross and blot themselves out in an act of complete dedication to the divine will. Both the figure of the Son of Man and the Servant are, as we have seen, representative figures, and although Christ suffers alone and does that which it is beyond human power to accomplish, it is clear from the whole trend of His teaching, and from the gathering of twelve disciples who were to be the nucleus of the new People of God, as well as from the words uttered in the Garden of Gethsemane and at the Last Supper, that Jesus intended that men should have a part in His sacrificial offering. The injunction to abide and watch in the Gethsemane story (Mk 14³⁴; Mt 26³⁸, omitted by Lk) suggests that He desired that His disciples should be with Him in order that they might enter into His redemptive activity in so far as they were able to do so. Further, the saying 'Watch and pray, that ye enter not into temptation' (Mk 14³⁸; cf. Mt 26⁴⁰ᶠ· and Lk 22⁴⁵ᶠ·) suggests that the disciples are being warned against failing to share in the loyalty and obedience of their Master.[8]

The Supper Sayings indicate even more clearly that Jesus intended that men should share in His redemptive activity. It

[8] cf. a full treatment of these sayings in Vincent Taylor, *Jesus and His Sacrifice*, pp. 150ff. For the Supper Sayings, cf. ibid., pp. 118-39.

THE DOCTRINE OF GOD

is significant that, whether or not the Supper was a Passover, a communal meal which could not be dissociated from the thought of the Passover took place in full view of His approaching death.[9] The terms 'body' and 'blood' in the Supper Sayings were metaphorical and indicated the life of complete obedience to be offered for men. The action at the Supper—the giving of the bread and wine to those who were with Him—clearly meant that the life that was to be surrendered should be received by the disciples. He would thus live in them and they would live in Him. Their discipleship was to consist, not in the 'imitation of Christ' or the pursuit of a moral ideal, but in active participation in the redemptive sufferings of Christ. They sat at the supper as the people of God, the members of the new order, founded like the old by sacrifice. Jesus united Himself afresh to them and equipped them for a ministry that was to be a continuation of His own. Their ministry would be dependent upon Him, and its abiding power would be the life that was obedient unto death. If there is to be a dying with Christ, there is to be a rising with Him and a final victory over the powers of evil. Jesus speaks of the Supper as a Messianic banquet (Mk 14[25], Lk 22[18, 29f.])—'I will no more drink of the fruit of the vine, until that day when I drink it new in the kingdom of God'. He looked forward at that hour to the Kingdom as established, and pictured the Messianic Feast as the place where those who had shared in His redemptive ministry would share in the final triumph.

We have been concerned in this chapter with the doctrine of God implied by the teaching of Jesus about the Kingdom of God. It has become clear that God is conceived as living and personal. He is known by His mighty works. He reveals Himself in and through the events of history. In the Old Testament we have the story of God visiting and redeeming His people who are estranged from Him by sin. In a series of historical crises, He declares His judgement upon sin and His purpose to redeem His people from their sin. Revelation and redemption are thus united in one process. God reveals Himself as Judge and Redeemer, and His judgement is an essential part of His redemptive purpose. Revelation is thus God Himself in redemptive action. It reaches

---

[9] *The Lord's Supper in the New Testament*, A. J. B. Higgins (*Studies in Biblical Theology, No. 6*), deals with current discussions and account is taken of the more important works on the subject by British and Continental scholars.

its climax in the life, death and resurrection of Christ. The coming of Christ was an event in history, but it differs from every other event, since it constitutes the meaning of all the events which went before. In Christ, the Kingly Rule of God was manifested in its redemptive power, and it was supremely manifested in the Cross which proclaims the judgement of God and the immeasurable power of His love for mankind. Who then is Jesus Christ? What does the teaching of Jesus about the Kingdom imply about His person?

CHAPTER THREE

THE PERSON OF CHRIST

THE Christian Church is built upon the conviction that the eternal Son of God was made flesh in the person of Jesus Christ who was truly God and truly man. An examination of the teaching of Jesus about the Kingdom of God indicates that this conviction, far from being a speculation of Christian Fathers and theologians, has its basis in the consciousness of Jesus Himself. We recall the titles which our Lord adopts for Himself, His sense of a unique relation to God, the absolute demands which He makes upon men, and the assumption that He is the pivot of human history, the arbiter of human destiny and the instrument of human redemption. He comes proclaiming the Kingdom of God, but unlike the prophets He proclaims the Kingdom as already present in Himself. He conceives Himself to be God's Messiah, called to offer to men the blessings of the divine Rule, and at the end of the age to enter upon the kingship which He was to receive from His Father, by treading the path of humiliation and death. He moulds His life and teaching, as we have previously observed, in such a way as to enable men to accept the gift that He brings. The Cross was not the condition of the coming of the Kingdom, but the redemptive agency of the Kingdom which had already come in the person of the Messiah. Thus the Jesus of history does not appear before us in the Synoptic Gospels in the role of a divinely inspired prophet. He comes rather as the fulfilment of Old Testament prophecies; as the divine Agent of God's kingly Rule, which brings deliverance from the power of evil, the forgiveness of sins and eternal life; as the Redeemer who voluntarily dies upon the Cross in obedience to the will of God; and as the Risen Lord who robs death of its ancient victories.

This, then, is the conception of Jesus Christ underlying the teaching of the Synoptic Gospels, and it implies the doctrine of the Incarnation, which still challenges human thought. How can Jesus be truly God and truly man? The reality of His humanity is not today a live issue, although there have been periods in the history of doctrine when it has been necessary for the Church to affirm that He was truly man. What perplexes us is the claim that He is God and man, and that in Him we have to do, not with a man who somehow became divine, but with a divine being who became human. It is important that the question should be thus bluntly stated, since it is possible to avoid the crucial difficulty by restatements of the Catholic doctrine which recognize no fundamental difference between God and man.

The classical solutions of the problem of the person of Christ made use of the concepts of Greek philosophy which were ready to hand and generally acceptable to theologians and philosophers —a situation that is not paralleled in contemporary thought. The Church owes a great debt to Greek thought and, if the time has come to seek a more adequate framework than that which later Greek philosophy provided, our obligation remains unchanged. It must, however, be borne in mind that Greek thought lacked an adequate conception of personality, and that the Church, in the development of its Christology, had therefore to work with concepts which may have served to safeguard the facts that called for explanation, but which were ill fitted to interpret their significance. The conception of substance which is enshrined in the formula 'of one substance with the Father' derives from the notion that certain things were alike and might be called by a common name because they possessed a common quality which was regarded as an independent object or substance. Thus arose the belief in independent qualities—whiteness, goodness, justice, beauty—which were present in particular objects. Divinity was held to be a substance and so was humanity. Humanity was a substance which was present in all human beings and divinity was a substance in which a divine being inhered. These two substances were believed to be fundamentally different, since divinity was eternal and unchangeable, whereas humanity was subject to change and perishable. Salvation thus could only be effected by the infusion of the eternal substance into the substance which was doomed otherwise to perish.

The philosophy known as logical realism, or the belief in the existence of independent qualities or substances over and above particular objects, encouraged the idea of an impersonal human nature, and created such a gulf between God and man as to preclude, on its own assumptions, the possibility of a genuine Incarnation. Further, the concept of substance obscured the nature of God as living, dynamic, and active in history, and its defects are further seen in the view of redemption as the infusion of our human nature by the divine, which may so easily be interpreted as meaning the deification of human nature.

The Chalcedonian Formula affirms that Jesus Christ is to be acknowledged in two natures, 'the property of each nature being preserved and concurring in one person and one hypostasis'. As the later Church saw, this doctrine, which is a brave attempt to express with its limited philosophical and psychological sources the real humanity and real divinity of Jesus together with His essential unity, involves two wills, one human and the other divine. While, however, we employ such categories as essence, substance, and nature, it is perilously easy to obscure this crucial issue. We are indeed involved either in postulating two wills in Jesus, or in adopting the theory of an impersonal human nature which has as its subject God the Son. It is not possible, on the analogy of the empirical ego and ultimate or transcendental ego of which some modern psychologists speak, to maintain the view that there was in Jesus a 'personality' which manifested itself in history as distinct from his 'person' which was divine.[1] Apart from other considerations which indicate that the analogy is defective, we are left wondering how it is possible for us to explain the prayers of Jesus and the conflict in the Garden of Gethsemane, if the hidden subject of the experience of Jesus was God the Son. An attempt is sometimes made to resolve the mystery by recourse to the view that in Jesus human nature was taken up into the Godhead, and thus man became fully personal. But this theory, which has been ably expounded by Dr H. M. Relton,[2] leaves us wondering whether the subject in this union or subsumption is still God the Son. If so, it is difficult to see what is to be gained by the substitution of the theory of '*anhypostasia*' (impersonal human nature) for that of '*enhypostasia*' (in-personal human nature).

It is not surprising that ways of interpreting the person of Christ have been explored which avoid some of the pitfalls to which the early history of Christology bears witness. The interpretation of the person of Christ in the light of divine immanence, or the belief that God is present in nature and in men in varying

[1] Brunner, *The Mediator* (1927), pp. 265ff. (E.T.),   [2] *A Study in Christology* (1922).

degrees, would seem at first sight to remove many difficulties, and to eliminate the seemingly fruitless issues which have exercised the minds of theologians, to the confusion of the laity, throughout the centuries. God, so it is submitted, who is present everywhere is supremely manifest in Christ because He yielded complete obedience to the will of God. Jesus was perfect man and may thus be described as the incarnation of God. There are, however, certain considerations which render this view profoundly unsatisfactory. First, it cannot be harmonized with the implications of the teaching of Jesus about the Kingdom of God. The interpretation which He placed upon His vocation, His consciousness of a unique relation to God, and His conviction that in His life and ministry the Kingdom had come and that the destiny of men was to be determined by their attitude to Himself, suggest that it is not enough to say that He was perfect man—and nothing more—or the flower of human evolution. Secondly, the starting point of human perfection is the forgiveness of sins. Jesus differed from us in His humanity, since He had no sin to confess. His communion with God was not based, as ours is, on the forgiveness of sins. Thirdly, human perfection is the result of a process of 'becoming'. Jesus did not become perfect. At every stage His whole being was controlled by the divine will. It is not suggested that His temptations were unreal or that He was exempt from the law of growth, but that He passed from one order of perfection to another. Every experience became a medium for the revelation of the perfection of His obedience. Fourthly, perfect man cannot become God. While there is kinship between man and God, and the doctrine of divine immanence has served to remind us forcibly of this fact which is an essential element in the doctrine of the Incarnation, there is a gulf fixed between man and God which human perfection cannot remove.

The Ritschlian school, which still exerts considerable influence, sought to commend Jesus and His Gospel of the Kingdom of God by dissociating the Christian Faith from metaphysics and the disintegrating effects of New Testament criticism, study of the history of religion, and scientific materialism. Ritschl believed that the problem of the 'two natures' and the relation of the Son to the Father in Trinitarianism had no vital connexion with Christian experience. He contends that we shall come to see the divine quality of the person of Christ only when we view Him in the light of what He has done. Jesus perfectly fulfilled His vocation, which was to establish the Kingdom of God. By His obedience to the divine will, He has realized in His own life a new relation between man and God which He is able to impart to all believers. Thus He has for us the value of God, and we shall but obscure the issue if we attempt to raise the metaphysical question as to who He was, or assess His significance in any other way than by reference to the relationship in which He stands to those who by faith in Him have found forgiveness and fellowship with God.

While Ritschl[3] expresses with admirable clarity the conviction so deeply embedded in the teaching of Luther and Schleiermacher that the person of Christ must be considered in the light of His work, his approach has serious defects that have given rise to Christological consequences which he did not intend. If Jesus brings to men pardon and peace, if His functions are divine, if, in the familiar phrase of Hermann, to call Him divine is only to give Him his right name, must we not go farther and ask: 'Who then is Jesus Christ?' and 'What is His relation to the universe?' Can we avoid indefinitely the question whether Jesus can have the value of God unless He is divine? Ritschl's insistence upon the interpretation of the person of Christ solely in terms of value judgements led in fact, in his own writings and in the development of the Ritschlian movement, to a conception of Christ that is as unsatisfying for religious experience as it is for philosophy. Although we still need to be reminded that our starting-point in Christology is the historic revelation and its interpretation in the redeemed life of the Christian community, it is significant that Ritschl speaks with reserve and some measure of reluctance about the pre-existence and exaltation of Christ. He does not deny the truth of either conception, but for him it is no part of the content of His divinity. He fails to recognize that the doctrine of pre-existence witnesses to the Incarnation not as an episode but as the self-giving of God which springs from His eternal nature. Further, although he is concerned to safeguard the uniqueness of the Christian revelation, the fundamental difference between Christ and ourselves is left in doubt. His emphasis on the ethical obedience of Jesus and his submission that the deity of Christ is

[3] *Justification and Reconciliation* (E.T. of Vol. III), esp. Ch. 4.

capable of being imitated by His people suggest—and we would not use a stronger word—the view that Jesus was divine by reason of His perfect obedience to the will of God. The revelation of God which we discern in Him is thus another name for his ethical harmony with the Father's will.

In declining to work out the fuller implications of the historic revelation, Ritschl, for all his merits, presents us with something less than a conception of One who has the religious value of God, and the inadequacy of his approach is seen in the variety of views which are represented in the history of the Ritschlian movement. While there were those, of whom the most distinguished were Julius Kaftan and Haering, who advanced beyond a Christology based on value judgements alone to a confession of the deity of Christ, there were others including Harnack, Wendt, and Bousset, who regarded Him as the supreme example of faith, the pioneer of a new race, rather than as the object of faith. What proved unacceptable in the Gospel story to personal faith was too easily explained away, and the area of historic fact in the records was limited to that which it was supposed faith could appropriate.

An attempt to safeguard the true humanity of Jesus while retaining an unqualified confession of His deity has been made by the adherents of what is known as the Kenotic theory, which was first systematically expounded by Thomasius in the first two volumes of his book: *Christ's Person and Work: A Presentation of Evangelical Lutheran Dogmatics from the middle-point of Christology.* According to the Kenotic theory, Jesus was the eternal Son of God, who surrendered His divine attributes (omnipotence, omniscience, omnipresence) in order that He might become man. Thus His humanity was genuine, although He was one with the Father as the second person of the Trinity. Here the love of God is supremely revealed, since the Son consents to become like us that He may reconcile us to God. Thomasius believed that he had succeeded in safeguarding what had in different ways been imperilled by Alexandrine and later Lutheran theology on the one hand, and the Antiochene and Calvinist theology on the other. He claimed, that is, to have found a satisfying conception of the God-man who is divine and human, without recourse to open or veiled dualism.

Although the theory is, in different forms, held by a number of British theologians belonging to our own time, it fails to yield a tenable approach to Christology. It assumes that apart from the historic revelation of God in Christ we know what God is like, and that the divine attributes which are not manifested in the Gospel record must, presumably, have been laid aside. Thomasius distinguished between immanent and relative attributes and thus prescribed the limitations of the incarnate life. Although we are presented with a picture of Jesus as a man, we are left asking what precisely was the relation of the human Jesus to the Eternal Son, and in what sense was the life of the Incarnate a revelation of the nature of God? If He divests Himself of His divine attributes, He ceases to be divine, whether or not the subject of His experience is regarded as divine or as human. And if when Jesus left the earth He abandoned His human nature, we have to inquire whether the human nature was taken up in some way into the life of the Godhead, or whether it was set aside as a temporary phase of the life of the Eternal Son. The Kenotic theory illustrates the extreme danger of bringing to the Gospel record certain preconceptions about the nature of God, instead of allowing our thought of God to be determined by the content of the historical revelation of God in Jesus Christ.

In recent years, Christology has been related to the study of the meaning of history and the problem of human existence. Thinkers whose general theological position is by no means identical speak of Christ as the centre or middle-point of history, a conception which Cullmann has impressively expounded in his work *Christ and Time*.[4] According to Cullmann, the coming of Christ is the centre of history. The primary emphasis in Christianity is not upon the future, as in Judaism, but upon the once-for-all event—the death and resurrection of Christ. The faith of the New Testament rests upon a victory already won and a fulfilment that has already come to pass. And yet, although the decisive battle has been fought, the war, as Cullmann says, may go on for a long time before the final Victory Day arrives. Christ reigns in the new age which His advent has inaugurated, but His lordship is hidden, and the veil will not be lifted until the present rule of Christ yields to the final coming of the Kingdom of God.

Barth,[5] again, holds that the death and resurrection of Christ mean the end of the old time of this sinful world and usher in the time of Christ, although, for the period between the first coming

[4] E.T. 1951.   [5] *Credo*.

of Christ and the making of a final end of history, Christians are still subject to the conditions of the old time. 'Realized eschatology', as interpreted by C. H. Dodd,[6] implies that the end of history has been revealed in Christ, but history still goes on. The triumph of the divine purpose disclosed in the myth of '*Doomsday*' has already been attained in the concrete historical event of the death and resurrection of Jesus Christ.

We may welcome the conviction which is central to these writers that Christ is the centre of history, but we need to beware of drawing inferences from this approach of which they, at any rate, would not approve. It is sometimes urged that the Christological issue must be delivered from metaphysical abstractions as well as from the question of the historicity of the particular events recorded in the Gospels, and seen against the background provided by the conflict between the Christian and secular interpretation of history. Bultmann, for example, in *Theology of the New Testament* (Vol. I), reaffirms the radical treatment of the Gospels as history which is found in his earlier works on *History of the Synoptic Tradition* and *Jesus and the Word*: the Baptism, Peter's confession and the empty tomb are legends, and Jesus did not believe himself to be the Messiah, nor did He conceive of Himself as coming again. Indeed, it would appear that we know almost nothing of the life and personality of Jesus. The New Testament on Bultmann's view needs to be demythologized, and by 'mythology' he means the 'use of imagery to express the otherworldly in terms of this world and the divine in terms of human life'.[7] What is needed in relation to the New Testament, so we are told, is a drastic unclothing of its mythological interpretation so that its essential message may be communicated to the present age. Bultmann believes that the existentialism of Heidegger, with its emphasis on the state of anxiety identified with guilt whereby man recognizes that he is hemmed in by death and cannot escape the forces ranged against him by his own strength, serves as the key to the interpretation of the New Testament message and to human experience as a whole. The meaning of the Resurrection in its demythologized form is that God has overcome sin and death, and the faith of Easter is faith in the word of preaching which brings illumination.

[6] *The Parables of the Kingdom, The Apostolic Preaching, History and the Gospel.*
[7] *Kerygma and Myth* (1953), p. 10 (note 2).

THE PERSON OF CHRIST 75

Paul Tillich,[8] again, endeavours to discover an approach to Christology, which is not dependent on such questions as the relation between the two natures in Christ and the historical authority of the Gospel 'events', but which will speak to man in this condition of estrangement and anxiety from God in which he finds himself. He would strip Christology of its mythical framework, and for him, in true Hegelian fashion, what signifies is that the Christian message about one who is human and divine is a symbol of the meaning of history. The question as to the relation of 'the God-Man' to Jesus of Nazareth is seemingly of no importance. Tillich begins with the questions men are asking about themselves and their existence in this world, and he considers that the two fundamental problems which man has to face are death and guilt. The formulation of these questions determines his interpretation of the person of Christ, and he imagines that they can be dissociated from historical criticism and from the issues which occupy such a prominent place in the history of the doctrine of the person of Christ. Like Bultmann he is concerned with the problem of communication, and he looks to the philosophy of existentialism combined with the biblical message for a solution.

There are three observations to be made here. First, 'demythologizing' in some form is necessary, and the history of Christian thought is almost a continuous illustration of the process. Christian truth needs to be put in new contexts, and it is an obligation from which there is no discharge to seek images or myths which convey to each succeeding age the nature of the Christian message. No doubt many of the symbols and figures used in the New Testament are unintelligible to our contemporaries, but the question may well be asked: at what point does myth in the sense of symbolic expression by which the divine is expressed in terms of this world pass over to myth in the sense of fictitious conception or event? When Bultmann has concluded his demythologizing process, what is there left to clothe?

Secondly, if Christ is the centre of history, or if he is believed to be the answer given to the ultimate problems propounded by human experience at any point in history, the question of the historicity of the Gospels and of its central figure is of first importance. We may agree that event and interpretation are indissolubly joined

[8] *Systematic Theology* (1953), Vol. I.

in the Christian Faith, and that the historical events recorded in the New Testament, as in the Old, are regarded by the writers as related to the drama of redemption. In that sense, the Bible is not primarily concerned with objective historical occurrences, but with events which have significance for faith. But they are believed to be events which have their origin other than in the interpretation which is put upon them. Something happened in the concrete historical situation which created a crisis and compelled a decision. We are, indeed, driven back to a study of the historical documents, and, if it is found that those documents are untrustworthy, it must not be imagined that the word as preached to the faithful will continue to carry conviction. If Jesus is nothing more than a symbol of divinity or humanity of the God-Man, and if His death and resurrection are nothing more than mythological patterns, it is difficult to see how the belief that Jesus is the centre of history and the key to human experience can be maintained. It is seriously misleading to speak of the resurrection of Jesus as a victory over sin and death unless, on the very ground on which defeat seemed to be registered, Christ rose from the dead. A vision of Christ reigning in heaven is something different from the Easter Faith, which rests upon the conviction that He was raised up by God and appeared to His friends. The historic faith of the Church is not a substitute for the belief in the historicity of Jesus, and, if we are to justify a Christian interpretation of history, we need to remember that it rests upon the truth of the affirmation that in the historical Jesus God Himself became man.

Thirdly, however important it may be to keep before us the need for correlating Christology with the interpretation of history and the ultimate human predicament, the question of the relation of Christ to God and to man must not be side-tracked. Otherwise we shall fail to communicate the Christian message, and what we build up into new historical situations will be something other than the Christian Faith that God in Christ visited and redeemed His people. It is easy to become impatient with what appear to be barren speculations about the nature of Christ. If, however, these questions are regarded as irrelevant, the door will be left open for interpretations of history which have in them no distinctive element. Those who resist the claims of Christology too often fall back on the conception of Christ as the flower of the evolutionary process, the climax of the human story, the religious hero who at long last found the secret of life in fellowship with God. Here we have an approach which cannot be reconciled with the revelation of God to which the Bible bears witness. In the biblical story, God at a certain point of time went into action and came into the world in Jesus Christ. The past and the future are to be interpreted in the light of that central event. Take away the conviction that God was personally present in Christ and that in Him His kingdom has come into history in a sense in which it was not there before, and the Christian interpretation of history and human experience must give place to conceptions which resemble too closely evolutionist theories of progress to be sharply distinguished from them.

Some recent writers believe that some progress toward a communicable Christology may be made by availing ourselves of certain insights provided by modern psychology and philosophy. Dr W. R. Matthews, in a recent volume on *The Problem of Christ in the Twentieth Century* marked by independence of judgement and clarity of expression, considers tentatively how far some of the findings of modern psychology and the philosophy of organisms and patterns of events shed light on the doctrine of the person of Christ.

First, he considers the concept of '*libido*', that primitive psychic energy which is in a general sense sexual, and he suggests that it was a reality for Jesus. To deny it in the experience of Jesus would destroy to a large extent our belief in His true humanity. If, again, the possession of instinctive desires is not the consequence of original sin, we may hold that '*libido*' was in the personality of Jesus and that He was free from original sin. Secondly, he refers to the racial unconscious and links this conception with the person and work of Christ as having racial significance. If we all share in the racial unconscious, a new meaning attaches to the phrase, 'As in Adam all die'. But what of the phrase, 'In Christ'? Redemption, Dr Matthews thinks, must take place at the unconscious and conscious level, but he is unable to answer the question which he himself puts: How can Christ descend into the underworld of ourselves and reconcile us there to God? Thirdly, he refers to telepathy and extra-sensory perception. He believes that telepathy may shed light, not only on our Lord's knowledge of human nature, as indicating a mind with telepathic power raised to a power unknown among us, but upon His work as redeemer. The hidden rapport between selves, of which telepathy provides evidence, might suggest a way of understanding afresh the meaning of such statements as 'He bore the sins of many'. All barriers are down, and the thoughts, desires and emotions of all the world flow in, even though the conscious life is in control. Extra-sensory perception—perception of objects without the use of normal physical senses and without the operation of telepathy—suggests that there is an aspect of human personality not chained to the present moment which may transcend time. Finally, Dr Matthews examines the philosophy of organism and patterns of behaviour events. He inquires whether, if we think of the will of God as a perfectly coherent moving pattern of acts of will, a pattern not yet completed, there is any reason why this pattern could not also be the moving pattern of behaviour events which constitute the temporal and historical aspects of human life. It would then be God manifest in the flesh.

We must content ourselves with a few brief comments on the suggestions which are put forward by Dr Matthews. Although they constitute a courageous attempt to set the doctrine of the Incarnation in a new framework, one wonders whether he has succeeded in doing more than restating the question to be answered. The concept of '*libido*' cannot be said to contribute to our understanding of our Lord's human nature, although it may challenge us to inquire afresh what we mean by saying that He was tempted in all points like as we are. If Jesus was free from original sin, does that mean that we are born with a bias which He did not share? If so, His human nature was different from ours. Much depends on how we define that misleading term 'original sin'. If original sin is sin, it is necessary to go farther and speak of original guilt. We are all involved morally in the sin of Adam. But if by that is meant that we are responsible for that sin in the sense in which we are responsible for our own, we are emptying moral responsibility of an essential part of its meaning. That we are bound up in some sense with the sin of the race cannot be denied any more than we can deny the solidarity of goodness. It is also beyond dispute that we have a tendency, which has deep ramifications in the history of the race, to seek our own interests and to oppose the divine will. But although that tendency is so potent as to make sin highly probable, it does not make it inevitable. It would be as well to interpret original sin as a universal tendency in human nature to seek the ends of self-interest and in this tendency Jesus shared. The temptations in the wilderness and in Gethsemane bear witness to the moral conflict which He endures, and of Him alone can it be said that He was without sin. He possessed what is understood by the '*libido*', but He directed His instinctive energies (which are not of themselves evil, even if they are inclined to evil owing to the heritage of the past and the pressure of our environment) toward God and the doing of His perfect will.

The concept of the racial unconscious may serve to guard us against an unduly individualistic view of human nature and enable us to appreciate afresh, not only that Christ is related to the race, but that His redeeming power extends to the deepest levels of our being, even if we have no means of discovering how the unconscious can be redeemed by Christ. Telepathy and extra-sensory perception remind us of capacities which our Lord may have possessed in a unique degree, but they certainly, as Dr Matthews would admit, do not explain the depth or extent of His knowledge of what was in man. Further, although evidence of telepathy and extra-sensory perception is being accumulated, we are still as far from understanding the mechanism of these capacities as our predecessors in the field. It is, again, doubtful whether the philosophy of pattern behaviour and of the will as a pattern of events is likely to advance the study of Christology. There is a sense in which a personal life may disclose the pattern of the divine will, but this particular philosophy fails to do justice to human personality and does not help us to understand how it was possible for God to enter personally into human experience. The terminology is changed. The fundamental problem remains unsolved.

The teaching of Jesus about the Kingdom of God presupposes the doctrine of the Incarnation. That doctrine affirms that Jesus Christ is human and divine, that, while He had a human will and shared everything essential to our own human nature, God was personally present in His person and work. It is generally recognized that if Jesus is God incarnate, He represents a level of experience which far transcends our own, and it is vain to expect that the thought-forms of any age will be anything but inadequate expressions of His personality. The process of demythologizing, in the sense of reinterpreting Jesus in new categories, is and should be a continuous process, and it is essential that its course should not be impeded by retaining concepts and terms which have well served their day and generation. And yet, although an adequate Christology is beyond our reach, the highest reaches of Christian experience may provide some hint of the nature of the union between God and man in Christ Jesus. Attempts to interpret the personality of Jesus which rely upon the psychology of inspiration leave us with a mysterious man, but not with God incarnate. It may be that, as Dr D. M. Baillie suggests,[9] we have in the paradox of grace a clue to the meaning of the incarnation, particularly if we focus attention upon St Paul's conception of faith-union with Christ.

In the experience of faith-union, the relationship of the believer to Christ is one of communion of wills. There is no suggestion of absorption of personality in the sense that the individual believer ceases to be. The extent to which the idea of absorption prevails in the history of Christian mysticism is largely due to the influence of an alien philosophy, and to a failure to relate mystical experience to the norm of all Christian experience as contained in the New Testament. 'I live,' says St Paul, 'yet not I, but Christ liveth in me.' He does not become Christ—a thought that is abhorrent to every Christian—but he is in Christ, even if there are days which seem to indicate that he is 'out of' rather than 'in' Christ. His virtues, his thoughts, his purposes are those of Christ, and in so far as he is one with Christ, his life, with that of all those to whom he is joined by this relationship, is an extension of the life of Christ in the flesh. Faith-union with Christ is not the result of human achievement. It is of grace: He loved me and gave Himself for me. Hence it never becomes a relationship of equality. We never cease to call Him 'Lord', even when we are permitted to know Him as friend. He is other than we are, and in spite of the intimate union that is experienced, the gulf between Christ and those who are in Him remains. In the experience of faith-union, Christ is transcendent and immanent, and His dealings with those who respond to His call are fully personal. Faith operates throughout and it implies in the first place an act of trust in the grace of God as revealed in Christ. But though that act is constantly renewed, it manifests itself in ethical obedience, in a sharing of the sufferings of Christ, in an ever-widening vision

[9] *God was in Christ* (1947), V.106ff.

of His purpose for us and for the world, and an ever-deepening assurance of growth in perfect love. But all is of Christ. Faith is His gift and the power to meet His absolute demands comes from Him, so that there are moments when the relationship may be so intense as to imply that He alone is the subject of our experience. 'I live . . . yet not I.' In faith-union personality finds its completion, and it is at the highest level of human attainment that we must look for the clue to the person of Christ.

Can we at any rate glimpse in the experience of faith-union something of the relation between Christ and God? This experience is deeply embedded in the Synoptic tradition, although it comes to fruition in the maturest thought of St Paul. The Last Supper, as we have seen, is permeated by the covenant idea, and in the covenant which our Lord made with his disciples He imparted to them His own sacrificial life that they might share in it. Those who receive the gift enter, in so far as they are able, into a knowledge of the relation between God and Christ, through the revelation of the grace of God to them which has been made in Christ. It is vain to found our Christology on metaphysical conceptions which have no direct relation to Christian experience, and here Ritschl uttered a timely warning. Our starting-point is the grace of our Lord Jesus Christ toward us, and as He deals graciously with us, we see revealed the eternal relationship between Father and Son.

The relationship of the Father and the Son is truly personal. Jesus was a man and He had a human will. If we speak of Him as Man we must not understand that description to mean that His human nature was impersonal, or that He was numerically one with the Father. He prayed to God, and, as we have already had occasion to notice, His practice of prayer can only be explained on the ground that His humanity was real. At every stage He rendered obedience to the will of God. Throughout His ministry, we may believe, He was subject to temptation, and He distinguished between the Father's will and His own. He went to the Cross in obedience to the will of God. On the cross He quoted the words of a Psalm which was a prayer bearing witness in the hour of seeming dereliction to utter dependence upon God. And it is into the hands of God that He commended His spirit at the end. Jesus was a man. At once we begin to realize that even if we have to destroy all our existing categories we cannot stop there.

His union with God was unbroken. Hence the experience of Christ became the experience of God. His communion with God did not mean at any stage the surrender of His own will, other than in the sense of moral obedience, but there was an identity of purpose which enabled God to enter personally into His life and manifest His redeeming love to men. God was in Christ and Christ was in God. This means something other than that God is like Jesus, a statement which can be so easily taken to mean that the Incarnation has not taken place and that in Jesus we have no more than a picture of the Father in heaven. It will not suffice to say that God is like Jesus, unless, like Jesus, God has shared human experience and borne its pain. What we would affirm is that God was Himself in Christ, and through the perfect sonship of Christ manifested in obedience to the divine will, He revealed and fulfilled His redemptive purpose to the world once and for all.

The analogy of the paradox of grace, like every other analogy, takes us but a short distance, and it is not suggested that we have here anything but a small window through which we can gain a limited vision of that which can never be brought fully within our understanding. Dr Baillie[10] remarks that somebody may wish to press the question: Would any man who lived a perfect life be therefore and thereby God incarnate? Such a questioner, he replies, would indeed be a Pelagian, showing by his very question that he regarded the human side of the achievement as the prevenient, the conditioning, and the determinative. But would he? The point of the question is surely that if a Christian is able to say 'I live, yet not I', what is the fundamental difference between him and Jesus Christ? It must be recognized that while the experience of union with Christ must be our clue to the nature of the union of Christ with God, it is by no means a complete clue.

Progress in Christology depends, not only on the success of the quest for a more adequate intellectual expression of the nature of Christ, but upon exploring the meaning of the Incarnation in worship, in social relationships, and in world evangelization. When the truth of the Incarnation is set forth in the worship of those who are united to Christ by faith, we may expect new meanings to be revealed, and a growing understanding of the relationship between God and Christ, who has reconciled men by His love to His Father's will. To be in Christ is to have a part

[10] op. cit., p. 131.

with all His people in the life which Christ shares with God. The worship of the Incarnate Lord is creative of a social ethic in which personal relationships are dominant, and in which material things are gathered up into the purpose of divine love. As we seek to affirm by deeds the Lordship of Christ in the realm of social values, inspired by the conviction that He is Lord of the world in which those values are to be expressed, we shall become conscious of the need for a conception of Christ that is rich and spacious enough to embrace the triumphs of His advancing Rule. Finally, when the Church recognizes afresh the urgency of the call to unite in the proclamation of the Gospel to mankind, irrespective of race, class or creed, and is fully persuaded that in Jesus Christ there was given a final revelation of the redeeming grace of God, we shall behold the glory of God in the face of Jesus Christ through the eyes of those from many nations who have entered into His Kingdom, and as we attain to unity of faith in the fellowship of the one Body, our individual faith will be made secure.

CHAPTER FOUR

THE CHURCH

ONE of the most significant results of the movement known as 'biblical theology' has been the rediscovery of the doctrine of the Church. The distinction between Christianity and the Church, which still in fact survives, has been outmoded by the closer study of the Old Testament and the New. Behind that distinction there lurked a number of fallacies. First, it was assumed that the Kingdom of God was primarily a community based upon allegiance of individuals to the ethical principles of Christ. What signified was not membership of the Church, but loyalty to the Kingdom which was deemed to have supplanted the idea of the Church. Secondly, it arose out of a failure to recognize the corporate nature of the Christian Faith. Although the Kingdom was regarded as a community or as having a social reference, the main emphasis seemed to rest on the life of the individual Christian considered apart from his membership of the Christian community. The individualism of the nineteenth century was reflected unmistakably in the attitude of Liberal Protestantism to the idea of the Church. Though it would be unjust to say that Liberal Protestantism dismissed the conception of the Church as irrelevant or unauthentic, it was largely responsible for the tendency, so deeply rooted in the minds of many within and without the Churches today, to regard the Church as an appendix to Christianity, a kind of society to which a Christian may or may not belong. Nowhere are dogmatic prejudices coloured by contemporary economic and political thought more obvious than in the treatment or lack of treatment of the doctrine of the Church in the writings of some nineteenth-century Protestant theologians. Thirdly, the distinction between Christianity and the Church served, it was thought, to answer the charge so frequently made that Christianity had failed. That the Church had failed was not denied, but its failure did not in any way affect the truth of Christianity. The Church had obscured the nature of the Christian message, which was essentially a call to individual discipleship in the service of the

Kingdom of God conceived as an organization based on love. Fourthly, it should be noticed that even in evangelical circles which are in revolt against the approach of the theological liberalism of the last century, the Church has been too often regarded as an addendum. The essential element in Christian experience, so it is clearly implied, is a personal relationship to Jesus Christ as Saviour, and there is the suggestion that it is at a later stage that the believer enters the fellowship of the Church. A personal relationship to Christ is thus dissociated from the idea of the Church and it is not surprising that Liberal theologians and evangelicals should have become, unbeknown to themselves, allies in relegating the Church to the circumference of the Christian Faith.

The reconsideration of the teaching of Jesus about the Kingdom of God, reviewed against the background of the Old Testament, has led to a recovery of the doctrine of the Church which is of first importance, not only for biblical scholarship, but for the furtherance of the Gospel throughout the world. We have seen in an earlier chapter in which the more positive results of recent investigations into the idea of the Kingdom in the mind of Jesus were summarized, that while the Kingdom means primarily the Rule of God, it implies a community, and that Jesus Himself formed a new community which should be the object of His love and the instrument of His redeeming purpose. That community is continuous with the people of God in the Old Testament, and yet it is discontinuous, since the Kingdom has come with Christ, and the powers of the age to come are already dynamically manifest in Him and in those who are united to Him in the covenant which He has established. The Church is the new people of God. Kingdom and Church are therefore correlative terms. The Kingdom is not to be identified with the Church, and for the first three centuries of our era no such identification was made. It is the organ of the Kingdom, the expression of the divine life which was revealed in the life, death, and resurrection of Christ, and the anticipation of the fulfilment of God's eternal purpose in the final establishment of His Rule.

We may now proceed to examine more systematically the significance of the doctrine of the Church in the light of the meaning of the Kingdom of God in the Synoptic Gospels.

First, the Church has a supernatural origin—and let us retain the term 'supernatural' in spite of some of its less fortunate associations. It is the gift of God in Christ, and the result of His gracious call to men to enter into a personal relationship with Himself and to live under His Rule. To respond to that call is to find ourselves at one and the same time in fellowship with God and with His people. But the initiative lies with God. The disciples were called by Jesus, and His covenant with them was sealed by His blood. There is nothing in the Gospels to support the view that the Church is a voluntary organization, or association of individuals who have come together, as is often done, to take counsel as to how some common purpose may be most effectively advanced. The disciples were 'chosen', and they became the nucleus of the new people of God, the 'little flock' to which Jesus expounded the message that was to constitute their way of life and their mission in the world. They were linked by their call with Abraham, but the ultimate origin of the community in which they found themselves through their allegiance to Christ was in the eternal purpose of God. The Church owes its origin and its existence to the action of God. It is the object of His redeeming purpose and the organ of His rule in the world.

As a community which has its origin in the will of God, the disciples were committed to a way of life which was not of their own choosing, but of divine appointment. The ethical demands of Jesus upon those who had entered into the '*ecclesia*' of God were dependent for their fulfilment on the gift of divine power. The Remnant was called to live at the supernatural level as a society which was not of this world, and the teaching of Jesus presupposed that the divine resources were available for the 'little flock'.

At first sight, it seems strange that there should be so few references to the Spirit in the Synoptic Gospels.[1] Apart from the post-resurrection sayings (Lk 24^{49}, Mt 28^{19}), we have six sayings only, and they have been subjected to detailed investigation by many scholars. It may be admitted that the form of these sayings has been affected by the development of thought in the primitive Church. But we have reason to believe that in these sayings we

---

[1] Mk 3^{29}=Mt 12^{31} (cf. Mt 12^{32} with Lk 12^{10} for version in Q).
Mk 13^{11}=Lk 12^{12}. Lk 21^{15}=Mt 10^{20} (version in Q).
Mk 12^{36}. Lk 11^{13} (Mt 7^{11}). Lk 4^{18}.
Mt 12^{28}=Lk 11^{20}. Luke probably retains the earlier form.
Cf. Barrett, *The Holy Spirit and the Gospel Tradition* (1947), which contains a comprehensive review of the evidence; Flew, *Jesus and His Church*; Vincent Taylor, *The Doctrine of the Holy Spirit*, Lecture II (Headingley Lectures), 1937.

have a genuine tradition rather than the reflection of the beliefs of a later age. They imply when examined (i) that Jesus connected the idea of the Spirit with His mission, (ii) that the activity of the Spirit is manifest in inspiration and guidance, and (iii) that the operation of the Spirit is revealed in the words and acts of Jesus, and by implication is available for his disciples. It is of secondary importance whether, in the passage 'If I by the Spirit of God cast out devils', we read with Luke 'the finger of God', since the meaning is fundamentally the same. The Kingdom comes with power and the miracles are signs of the new energies now available for the overthrow of the powers of evil. All things are possible to them that believe and to those who ask it shall be given. It has been said that while the above saying, 'If I by the Spirit of God', brings together Jesus, the Kingdom, and the Spirit, there is nothing to establish a similar relation between the disciples, the Kingdom, and the Spirit.[2] But if there are few references to the Spirit, the availability of divine power is throughout implied.

The sayings of Jesus about the Spirit are admittedly few, and various explanations have been proposed. For example, it has been suggested by E. F. Scott[3] that the idea of the Spirit was uncongenial to Jesus, since it was bound up with the belief in intermediaries, as developed in later Judaism, which came between man and God and removed God to a distance. Apart from the fact that to think of God as Spirit is not necessarily inconsistent with the conception of Him as Father, the Gospels witness to the fact that Jesus accepted the current beliefs about spirits and demons and angels. Dr Vincent Taylor,[4] again, has urged that much in Apostolic Christianity in connexion with the Spirit, the Church, the Eucharist and the Cross had beginnings in sayings of Jesus about the Cross which passed out of recollection because they dealt with familiar and accepted things. But the view that the formation of the Gospel tradition was determined to a large extent by controversy needs to be treated with great reserve, and there were certainly other factors that must be taken into account of equal if not of greater importance. In any case the Acts suggest that there was controversy on the subject in relation to baptism. Dr Flew makes the fruitful suggestion that

---

[2] Barrett, op. cit., p. 159.   [3] *The Spirit in the New Testament* (1923), p. 79.
[4] *The Doctrine of the Holy Spirit*, pp. 53-55.

the Messianic secret offers a parallel to silence about the Spirit, since just as He rejected the titles which rested upon popular misconceptions of His mission, so He had to baptize the conception of the Spirit into His life and death.[5]

If by the Spirit we mean God Himself in action in the world and in the heart of man, then the whole ministry of Jesus is a ministry of the Spirit and the community which He founded is a fellowship of the Spirit. The full power of the Spirit could not be liberated until the work of Christ was completed. Just as the Kingdom is present and future, so is the power of the Spirit. The Spirit is manifested at every stage of the ministry of Jesus, and by His final act of obedience, followed by His resurrection, He brought within the reach of man all the redemptive energies of God. But during the earthly life of Jesus, the power of the Spirit, though partially veiled, was available for the disciples, and it was mediated through their unity in Christ.

The supernatural origin and nature of the Church is again reflected in its message. To the disciples had been revealed the 'mystery' of the Kingdom of God, and the word 'mystery' should be interpreted, not in the light of the pagan mysteries which represent in dramatic form what is hidden for the benefit of the initiated alone, but in relation to the Hebrew conception of self-revelation. The good news which Jesus proclaimed refers to the unveiling of the redemptive purpose of God. What makes the message good news is the affirmation that the secret counsel of God is now an open secret. The Kingdom has come with Christ. The New Age has dawned, and those who have eyes to see may behold the end of God's dealings with mankind in the person and work of Christ. As the ministry of Jesus proceeds, the 'mystery' is progressively unfolded, and after Cæsarea Phillipi He looks to the passion and the resurrection for the fuller and deeper manifestation of its meaning. As we have seen, the disciples, in so far as they were able, were called to share with Jesus in the cost of the passion without which the mystery of the Kingdom could not be finally disclosed. But the purpose which they were called to serve was not their own. It was the purpose of God, which had confronted them with an absolute demand in the person of Jesus Christ. The burden of their message as they went forth on a missionary tour, was not what they thought themselves about their

[5] *Jesus and His Church*, pp. 66-72.

Master, or what they had found to be true about God and the world. It was the proclamation of what God had done. The Kingdom of God has come upon you. God has in Christ visited His people in judgement and mercy, and the divine action is a challenge to repentance, which means not simply moral reformation but a turning or returning to God.

The *ecclesia*, then, is a community which has its source in the eternal will of God. Its power to rise to the moral and spiritual level required by life in the new age comes from God, and the message by which it is constituted is from above. It is a message about God and comes from God. It is proclaimed by God in the person of Christ and supremely in His death and resurrection.

Secondly, the Church which is the gift of God is a visible society.

If the Church is the organ of the Kingdom, the agent of God's kingly Rule, it must exist as a concrete entity in space and time. The Kingdom is from above, but it is manifested in history, since while the Rule of God is not to be identified with the processes of history, it is through events that it is made known. When we speak of the Church as a visible society, we mean that it is composed of people whose life is ordered in accordance with a particular pattern. The conception of the invisible Church has led to considerable confusion of thought about the true nature of the Church, although in view of the seeming decline of the Church in the world and the failure in faith and practice of many of its members, it is not surprising that there should have emerged the idea of the Invisible Church as the society of the elect. But the concept, unless it refers to the communion of saints in heaven, has no warrant in the Gospels or the rest of the New Testament, and when pressed, promotes a false individualism and a type of spirituality which cannot be reconciled with the doctrine that the Word became flesh. There is no justification for the view that the visible Church is inherently a false representation of the Invisible Church, unless a debased Platonism is substituted for faith in the Incarnation.

Those such as Emil Brunner who repudiate the distinction between the visible and the invisible Church are in danger of rehabilitating it in their thought. In his *Misunderstanding of the Church* he reminds us that the Church is a historically evolved form, a vessel of the *Ecclesia*, 'which is the oneness of communion with Christ by faith and brotherhood in love'.[6] The promise of invincibility and eternal durability is given, not to the Church as an institution, but to the *Ecclesia* alone, whose ancient framework may be destroyed and its place taken by structures of a very different order. With this familiar thesis there would be a considerable measure of agreement in many churches. Behind it, however, seems to be the assumption that the structure of the Church, or its particular shape, is external, and that its essential nature is independent of its historic expressions. 'In spite of everything,' we read, 'the institutional Church has shown itself to be the most powerful *"externum subsidium"* of the Christian communion, from the days when the struggle with the heresies and fanaticisms of gnosis caused the *Ecclesia* to establish its monarchical episcopate and its quasi-political structure, even to our own times when, in its fight against the totalitarian state of Hitler, the dynamic Christian communion experienced once more the protection and the stability which the official Church was able to offer it'.[7] Now it may be readily admitted that in the teaching of Jesus we have nothing more than the germ of a ministerial order, that in the New Testament as a whole there is no constitution enjoined which is to be determinative for the Church in perpetuity, and that to regard the structure of any one particular communion as final may well result in obstructing the movement of the Holy Spirit within the Universal Church. We must, however, recognize that the structure of the Church cannot be regarded as merely external, any more than the body of our Lord could be so regarded. One of the implications of the doctrine of the Incarnation is that the physical ceases to be merely external and becomes sacramental. To speak of the Church as a vessel of the *Ecclesia*, and as an '*externum subsidium*', suggests that it is possible to conceive of the Christian Church as an invisible society, whereas it is only known to us as a visible and historic body. 'The New Testament *"Ecclesia"*', writes Brunner, 'the fellowship of Jesus Christ, is a pure communion of persons and has nothing of the character of an institution about it; it is therefore misleading to identify any single one of the historically developed churches, which are all marked by an institutional character, with the true Christian communion.'[8] It is certainly misleading to identify any one of the historic churches with the one holy

[6] op. cit., p. 118.   [7] ibid., p. 116.   [8] ibid., p. 17.

THE CHURCH 91

Catholic Apostolic Church to the exclusion of others, but it is not on the ground of its institutional character that any Church fails to be the true Christian communion. From the very beginning, the fellowship of the Church had a visible form, which expressed of its true life and served to mediate that life to men. Our Lord was baptized as He entered upon His ministry, and at its close He shared with His disciples in that meal which has become central in the life of the Christian Church. While the fellowship of Jesus and His disciples was simply organized, it had visible marks. Jesus sent them out to proclaim the Good News; He taught them how to pray, and set before them the meaning of the Rule of God in relation to their fellow men and the created order. Jesus left behind him no system of doctrine, no instructions for the organization of the ministry, no detailed guidance about worship. He did, however, leave a community of persons which came to be known by its continuance 'in the apostles' teaching and fellowship, the breaking of bread, and the prayers'. These words describe a very simple structure, but it is a structure (or order). Faith and order can only be separated by misrepresenting both.

It may be that the unwillingness to recognize the institutional character of Christian fellowship is to be traced to the identification of structure with ministerial order, and to the doctrine that a certain type of ministerial order is an essential mark of the true Church. Preoccupation with the question of a valid ministry is calculated to obscure the nature of the Church as the people of God who are called to set forth the Rule of God in the world. The Church has certain structural qualities which do not change from age to age. It is marked by the preaching of the Word, the observance of the sacraments, instruction in Christian truth, unity and continuity with the faith of the Apostles, communion with Christ in worship and daily life, and obedience to the Rule of God in all human relationships. What we need to observe is that while the Church is necessarily institutional in character, some elements in its structure are, or may be, transient, whereas others are permanent. Unity and continuity are indispensable marks of the Church, but the onus of proof lies upon those who claim that episcopacy, as the bond of unity and continuity, is indispensable to the Church for all time. The repudiation of this claim, however, should not be taken to mean that structure is unimportant or that faith should be sharply distinguished from order. If the Church is the body of Christ on earth, it must have a visible and clearly defined form, so that it may be the expression of God's purpose for this world and the instrument of His Kingly Rule.

The true context of the Church is the Kingdom of God which has already come on the stage of history in Jesus Christ and His acts of redeeming love, and which is to be consummated in the final vindication of the end to which history, under the judgement and mercy of God, is moving. The Church is the organ of the Kingdom, and it is in the light of the kingdom that its structure must be judged. Too often discussions about the unity of the Church are related almost exclusively to the necessity of safeguarding sound doctrine and the historic continuity of the Christian fellowship. Hence the episcopacy becomes the major concern, and the structure of the Church is conceived as being determined by the ministry. The idea of the Church as the people of God is thus obscured, and the Church and episcopacy tend to be regarded as synonymous terms. If the Church is to fulfil its divine function, it must keep in full view the absolute claims of the Kingdom of God. It exists to proclaim the kingly Rule of God in the world, and to set it forth in a way of life that includes the redemption of personal, economic, and political relationships. The institutional character of the Church must thus be taken to include, not ministerial order alone, or indeed chiefly, but the visible expression in human relationships, at the spiritual, ethical, and social level, of that Kingship which is the source and criterion of its message and mission.

Thirdly, the Church is apostolic. Though the term 'apostle' in the New Testament seems to fluctuate between a more rigid and more general use, the title of the 'twelve' to be called apostles is undisputed. There is evidence in the Gospels that they were so called. In Mark 3^{14}, we read: 'And he appointed twelve, that they should be with him, and that he might send them forth to preach, and to have power to heal sicknesses, and to cast out demons.' Mark describes their mission in 6^{7-13} (Lk 9^{10}), and describes the disciples upon their return from their mission as apostles. Professor Manson suggests that the picture of the followers of Jesus as given in the Gospels is one of a series of concentric circles. There were those on the outer circles who were impressed

THE CHURCH 93

by the teaching of Jesus and who sought his help. Again there were those who went a step farther and responded to the call for repentance and faith. Finally there were the smaller groups like the Seventy (-two) and the Twelve, and within the Twelve there were three who stood in a specially intimate relation to Jesus.[9]

What was the place of the 'twelve' in the ministry of Jesus? They were called by Christ and commissioned by Him to act as His agents. The Hebrew term *'shaliach'* (the verb is *'shalach'* and is translated by *'apostellein'* in the Septuagint) may shed some light on the meaning of the term 'apostle'. A *shaliach* was an official who was authorized to act on behalf of someone else. Hence, in the familiar Rabbinic maxim, 'A man's *shaliach* shall be as himself'. The commission which he received could not be transferred to another, and the word describes not so much an official status as a legal function to be discharged on behalf of an individual or corporate body.

There are important similarities and even more important differences between the *sheluchim* and the apostles. The latter were the personal representatives of Christ, commissioned by Him to do His work. They were given authority to act on His behalf, but their authority, as in the case of the *shaliach*, was personal and could not be transferred by them to another. But what determines the nature of the apostleship is the fact that the call comes from Christ, and that it was a call to share in His ministry so that men might repent and believe the Gospel. So far as is known, there was among the *sheluchim* no missionary activity, though there may have been religious activity directed to the Jews alone.

There is nothing in the Gospels to suggest that the twelve were appointed to any office. The passage in which the sons of Zebedee ask that they should be assigned special places and privileges (Mk 10[37]) implies the absence of an official hierachy in the community which Jesus had gathered. In the Kingdom of God there is only one law and that is the law of service and sacrifice (Mk 10[42ff.]). The famous passage following upon Peter's confession at Cæsarea Philippi (Mt 16[17ff.]) has been the subject of interminable discussion, and it is doubtful whether it sheds much light on the peculiar position of Peter in the community or on the nature of the Church. If the passage is to be regarded as genuine, even

[9] *The Church's Ministry* (1948), p. 47.

though the original setting may have been displaced, we may conclude, among the alternative interpretations offered, that the Rock is Peter himself rather than his confession, that he is conceived of as the Grand Vizier of the Kingdom of heaven, and as a wise scribe who has authority to judge, and to allow and disallow certain courses of action. But, as has been frequently observed, the prerogatives promised Peter are in the rest of the New Testament granted also to others.[10] Further, we are not justified in assuming on the evidence before us that the Apostolate was restricted to the Twelve. The Twelve had an experience of Christ which was inalienable and could not be transferred. They had lived with Jesus and shared His companionship. But it is noteworthy that the account given by Luke of the mission of the Seventy (Lk 10[1ff.]) suggests that an authority similar to that granted to the twelve was given to a much larger group, and whether or not we have here a doublet of the mission of the Twelve, it is significant that the passage should have been included in this Gospel.

What, then, in the light of the Synoptic gospels are the characteristics of apostolicity?

First the apostles are called. The idea of a 'call', or the doctrine of election, is inseparable from the conception of God and His dealings with man as portrayed in the Old Testament and the New. It is illustrated in the establishment of a covenant between God and Israel, His people; and in the covenant made at the Last Supper its full meaning is set forth. The initiative lies with God, and He calls, not because those who receive the call are worthy to be His servants, but because they are the objects of His love. Hence the first mark of an apostle is that he has been called of Christ to His service.

The apostle is called out of the world—out of the 'present age' which is organized apart from God. Although he lives in the present age and serves God within it, he is in a real sense opposed to it. He is a citizen of the Kingdom of God and must stand in judgement upon a way of life which is a denial of the divine will. Hence to be 'called' means a life of holiness, or separation unto God. The apostle represents a distinctive order, since here and now he lives by the light and in the power of the eternal rule of

---

[10] cf. R. Newton Flew, *Jesus and His Church*, pp. 123ff. Cullmann, *Peter, Disciple, Apostle, Martyr*, Part II (E.T.).

God which has come with Christ. Otherworldliness is thus the mark of the apostle. No quality of character has been more grievously misunderstood. So often it is identified with a negative morality, or with a spurious kind of piety which is unrelated to the material world and to human society, and which is inspired solely by the desire for future salvation. Those who were called by Christ and taught by Him the way of the Kingdom were in no danger of yielding to this caricature of apostolicity. Otherworldliness, it is true, has its negative aspect. We are accustomed to say that the Christian ethic is positive whereas the Ten Commandments are negative. It is forgotten that a positive ethic implies a negative attitude, or the determination to say 'No', to thought and conduct which cannot be reconciled with the way of life to which we stand committed. Those whom Jesus calls are inevitably strangers in this world, not because they are seeking to escape from life or to express their faith other than through the sphere of service which this life in its ordinary relationships provides, but because the world which was made for the glory of God has been defaced by the sin of man. They are thus called out of its false values and judgements, still to live within it, but as sons of a kingdom which is not of this world. All their thinking and all their doing are submitted to the judgement of the divine Rule.

The apostle is called to enter into a personal relationship with Christ and to share in His ministry. 'And he appointed twelve, that they might be with him' (Mk 3¹⁴). It is only after they have been with Him and gained an insight through His personal companionship and teaching into the nature of His mission that they are sent forth to preach. Their preaching and their way of life are determined, not by the external imitation of their Master or by a valiant effort to put the 'principles' of His teaching into practice, but by the new fellowship with Him and with one another into which they have entered. They enter into that fellowship by faith. They are confronted by Christ who calls them out of the world into the new age which has dawned with His coming. Although in the new age they have a part in His ministry and share in His fellowship, He remains to the end the object of faith. While there is parity between the disciples, there is no parity between the disciples and their Lord. He calls and they are the chosen.

Secondly, the apostles are sent forth. They are sent forth as the representatives of their Lord. We recall the Rabbinical dictum about the *shaliach*: 'A man's *shaliach* shall be as himself.' There are sayings of Jesus in all three Gospels which echo this maxim. In Mark 9^{37} (cf. Mt 18^5; Lk 9^{48}) we read: 'Whosoever shall receive one of such children in my name, receiveth me; and whosoever shall receive me, receiveth not me, but him that sent me.' In Matthew 10^{40} we read with special reference to the disciples: 'He that receiveth you receiveth me, and he that receiveth me receiveth him that sent me.' In Luke 10^{16} we have the form: 'He that heareth you heareth me; and he that rejecteth you rejecteth me; and he that rejecteth me rejecteth him that sent me.' Then again the same thought is found in Mark 9^{41}: 'For whosoever shall give you a cup of water to drink, because ye are Christ's, verily I say unto you, he shall in no wise lose his reward.'

The apostle goes forth with Christ to continue His ministry.[11] Throughout, the emphasis is upon the ministry of Christ—'He that heareth you heareth me. . . . He that rejecteth you rejecteth me'. It is Christ who is present in every proclamation of the Good News and in the healing of all manner of diseases. Hence, while there is a sense in which we may speak of the apostle as the representative of His Lord, the idea of 'representation' is not sufficiently intimate to describe the union between Christ and those whom He sends forth. The apostles are united to Christ by faith and it is Christ who dwells in them as they obey His call. It is His ministry that they serve, His message that they proclaim, His works that they do. While there may be an objection to the description of the Church as the continuation of the Incarnation, since it is composed of fallible and sinful men, that is what the Church is in the divine intention. It is Christ Himself going forth through the dedicated lives of His disciples whom He has united to Himself.

The Twelve were sent to proclaim the Kingdom of God and to have power to heal sicknesses and to cast out demons (Mk 3$^{14-15}$; Mt 10^1; Lk 9^1). It is to be observed that the authority to preach the Good News of the Kingdom is linked with the power to overcome the forces of evil in all their varied manifestations.

---

[11] For a singularly fresh treatment of the ministry of Christ in and through the Church as the one 'essential' ministry, see Manson, op. cit.

Preaching and healing are not to be regarded as disparate tasks. The Gospel that is preached is the Gospel of the Kingdom, and its manifestation in Christ means the victory over the kingdom of evil. The Kingdom has come with power, and its coming is the beginning of the end of everything that is opposed to the will of God. Again, as they go forth to announce the kingdom which has come and which will be consummated in the final victory of God, and to confront men with the powers of the new age which has already dawned as well as with the judgement on the 'present age' which the Kingdom of God brings in its train, it is Christ Himself, the Kingdom in action, who energizes within them. They bear His authority because they are in Him.

The range of the apostolic ministry is universal. It is well known that the question has often been discussed as to whether Jesus conceived of a universal mission. Professor Jeremias,[12] for example, contends that Jesus did no missionary work among the Gentiles and forbade it to his disciples; and that the gathering of the Gentiles is 'God's powerful eschatological action, the last great revelation of the unbounded grace of God'. While the case is overstated and the exegesis in places somewhat strained to suit his thesis, he calls attention once again to a problem which cannot be evaded. It is doubtful whether there would have been a dispute in the primitive Church about the admission of the Gentiles if our Lord's teaching on the subject as it was recalled had been unmistakably clear. We are not concerned to examine the question in detail, but to make three general observations which should be taken into account. First, our Lord's mission was primarily to His own people. He sought, as we have seen, to reconstitute the Old Israel and fit it for its task in the new age. Hence it was almost inevitable that His teaching might sometimes appear to be particularist rather than universal. To suggest, however, that Jesus was a particularist is to ascribe to Him a view of God which falls below the highest reaches of the Old Testament as it contemplates the mission of Israel. Secondly, the attitude of Jesus toward the ceremonial law indicates a universalistic outlook. One of the most revolutionary of the sayings of Jesus is Mark 7[18]: 'Do ye not perceive, that whatsoever thing

---

[12] *Studiorum Novi Testamenti Societas*, Bulletin III, 'The Gentile World in the Thought of Jesus'; cf. also Bulletin 1950, J. Munck, 'Israel and the Gentiles in the New Testament'; Cadoux, C. J., *The historic mission of Jesus* (1941), Ch. 5.

G

from without entereth into the man, cannot defile him?' said Jesus. And the words, 'This He said, making all meats clean', are fair comment. Thus the main barrier between Jew and Gentile was abolished, and the central emphasis in religion was made to rest on the relation of a man's inward disposition to God. Thirdly, if the ruling conception in the teaching of Jesus was the sovereign love of God, which was not dependent upon human merit or race or sex, the belief in a universal mission is necessarily implied. The ideal of Israel as God's agent for the bringing of the knowledge of God to the Gentiles must have been present to His mind as He pondered the Old Testament, and if it cannot be said that the universalistic element is stressed, the explanation is to be sought in His desire to avoid needless controversy and to equip His disciples for the task which the old Israel had declined. Had Jesus drawn out the full implications of the doctrine of God's unrestricted love, He would have deflected attention from the Gospel of God and converted His message into a political issue. The fruits of His reticence are seen in the rapid expansion of the Galilean Faith into a world-religion.

The Church is the extension or continuation of the earthly ministry of Jesus, and all its members are apostles, in the sense that they do not join the Church, but are called into its worship and service. They are commissioned to go forth as the people of God, to proclaim in their different ways the judgement and mercy of God revealed in the coming of the Kingdom, and to prepare the way for the final realization of the divine purpose in the establishment of God's kingly Rule. The apostles in the time of our Lord were not the nucleus of the ministry, since no official ministry existed, but of the New Israel, the people of God, in an age in which the powers of the age that was to come had already been made manifest. In the Primitive Church the 'twelve' had, as we have observed, a unique position due to an experience that was incommunicable, but in that Church there were varied ministries which were the possession of the Church as a whole, and which were bestowed upon it by the Spirit for the building up of the Body of Christ. Nowhere is there any ground for concluding that in the New Testament the ministry of the apostles, which was one of many ministries, constituted the *ecclesia*.

In the course of the history of the Christian Church, the

structure of the Church has undergone considerable development, and it would be generally recognized that, in view of the emergence of situations which could not be paralleled in the time of our Lord or in the primitive Christian community, it was inevitable that provision should be made for the formation of the Canon, the determination and establishment of doctrinal standards, preaching and teaching, worship and the due administration of the Sacraments, and the care of souls. The expansion of the life of the Church revealed the need for preserving unity and continuity with the faith of the apostles, and in the second century we see the rise of the doctrine that the supreme authority of the Church lies in the episcopacy. Today, in the sphere of ecumenical discussion, the issue before us is not whether the Church should have a structure which is organically related to its Faith, or whether there should be orders of ministries duly appointed to discharge their several functions, or whether the New Testament '*ecclesia*' is to be found in its fullness in any of the historic Communions, but whether the centralization of authority in the episcopal office is in harmony with the nature of the apostolate as described in the Gospels. In short, does the episcopacy constitute the indispensable historic link with the original apostolate, and is it essential to the unity of the Church and the proclamation of the Gospel?

It is not enough to point to the many benefits which the episcopate has bestowed and then refer to its historical perversions, any more than it is to acknowledge the fact that God has 'richly blessed the ministry of the Free Churches' and draw attention to their fissiparous tendencies. The structure of any Church, however defective, can be used by God for His glory. Nor again can we take refuge in the seemingly comfortable distinction between the fact of the episcopacy and its varied interpretations. In the Report of the Committee on 'The Unity of the Church' (Lambeth Conference 1930), the historical episcopate is defined in terms of succession in office and of consecration, and it is claimed that it can be traced back to 'the original conception of the Apostolic ministry', even if the history of the episcopate has sometimes obscured its historical purpose. 'What we uphold is the Episcopate, maintained in successive generations by continuity of succession and consecration, as it has been throughout the history of the Church from the earliest times, and discharging those functions which from the earliest times it has discharged.' It is clear enough that in this statement fact and interpretation are closely intertwined, and about the interpretation there has been considerable dispute. In particular, what is meant by 'the earliest times', and is it a fact or a theory that the historic episcopate is based upon the 'original conception of the Apostolic ministry'? There need be no dispute about the necessity of episcopal functions, which are discharged in different ways by different churches. But when it is implied that there can be no reunion apart from the recognition of the historic episcopate in its continuity of succession and consecration, the submission that no particular theory or interpretation of the episcopate is required as a condition of union is somewhat difficult to understand. The term 'historic episcopate' is itself highly ambiguous. Sometimes it is used in the above sense of continuity of succession and consecration, sometimes as meaning the historic transmission of the Apostolic commission through the episcopacy and sometimes as implying nothing but the element of historic continuity in the life of the Church. We are perhaps justified in asking what this elusive fact is that seems capable of such diverse interpretations.

Is there any criterion to which the development of traditional order can be referred? It is to the New Testament that we must turn; and while the activity of the Holy Spirit must be recognized in the formation of ecclesiastical tradition, we have to remember that the Holy Spirit takes of the things of Christ as recorded in the Scriptures and reveals them to us. Hence tradition must always be subordinated to the Scriptures. Unless the New Testament is regarded as our supreme authority, we have no objective authority by which we can test the authenticity of any traditional development in the history of the life and doctrine of the Church. If it is well attested that the original apostolate was *sui generis*, that our Lord did not establish anything that can be described as a ministerial order, that the marks of apostolicity are to be ascribed to the Church as a whole which is the continuing ministry of Christ and not to a particular order within it commissioned to transmit apostolic authority, that the authority of the Church is constituted by the revelation of the redeeming purpose of God in Christ, and that the nature and function of the Church are to be related to the Kingdom of God of which it is the divinely appointed organ, we are driven to the conclusion that the insistence on a succession of office and consecration, as an indispensable condition of the reunion of the Church of Christ and as the guarantee of the maintenance of pure doctrine, is a departure from, and not a development of, the witness of the Gospels and the rest of the New Testament.

It is not part of our purpose to deal with the vexed problem of reunion. We would, however, reiterate the conviction that if the nature of the Church and its ministry could be approached afresh in the light of its relation to the kingdom of God, present and future, as the manifestation of God's power in the mighty acts of redemption wrought in Christ, and as the final revelation of the divine glory in the triumph of the eternal Rule of God, we should have our feet firmly fixed on the road that is marked out for us in the Scriptures, and our continuity with the Church of the Apostles would be unmistakably established. The Church belongs to the interval between the Incarnation and the coming of Christ in the fullness of His power. As it seeks to preach the Gospel to all nations, in communion with the redeemed of all ages, it will find God's way of healing its divisions, and of expressing through its worship, fellowship and ministry, the unity which it already enjoys in Christ.

CHAPTER FIVE

THE CHRISTIAN HOPE

THE New Testament is governed by two inseparable convictions. On the one hand, there is the fixed belief that the end to which all history is moving has been manifested in the coming of Jesus Christ and in His victory over the powers of evil by His death and resurrection. On the other hand, there is the glowing expectation, rooted in the revelation of God's eternal purpose in Christ which was being increasingly verified in the experience of the Church, that earthly history in its existing form, with its limitations and frustrations, would yield to the coming of Christ in glory and the final establishment of the Kingdom of God. 'For our citizenship,' says St Paul, 'is in heaven; from whence also we wait for a Saviour, the Lord Jesus Christ: who shall fashion anew the body of our humiliation, that it may be conformed to the body of his glory, according to the working whereby he is able even to subject all things unto himself' (Ph $3^{20\text{-}1}$). The early Christians were persuaded that they were living in the age of fulfilment. They shared in a salvation already accomplished in Christ; they knew that the decisive battle in the conflict between good and evil had been fought, and that Christ by His resurrection from the dead was now divinely acclaimed as Lord of the universe. They were conscious of the infinite resources of the Holy Spirit, released by what God had accomplished by His redemption in Christ. They had been once and for all enlightened; they had tasted the excellence of the Gospel and the powers of the coming age.

And yet their eschatology, if 'realized', was veiled. The Kingdom that had come with Christ was to be consummated in the future, in the fullness of its power and glory. For them the Kingdom in its final fulfilment was associated with the coming of Christ. It is true that the phrase 'second coming' is not found in Scripture, but it represents a conviction deeply embedded in Scripture, whatever interpretation may be given to its origin and

THE CHRISTIAN HOPE 103

validity. Permeating the faith and life of the primitive Church was the hope that Christ, who ruled as King over the 'present age' by reason of His victory over the powers of evil, would appear as Judge, and that the present phase of human history would end and give place to the final coming of the Kingdom of God. With Christ would appear those who belonged to Him, and to them would be given a place in the consummation of God's kingly Rule.

The tension between the present and future fulfilment of the divine purpose served as a safeguard against undue preoccupation with the future and against the easy optimism of secularist dreams. From the existing scene, with its continuing warfare and manifest disabilities, the Church of the New Testament looked for a new heaven and a new earth, a transfigured universe in which the significance of all the preceding stages of human history would be gathered up. It was believed that the coming of the Lord would not be long delayed, although the Kingdom of Christ must continue within the present order until 'He has put all things under His feet' (1 Cor 15^{25}).

In the teaching of Jesus, we have sufficient evidence for the emergence of the Christian hope as found in the Primitive Church, and even if much remains obscure, there are certain affirmations about the consummation of the Kingdom and the coming of the Son of Man which may with a measure of confidence be made.

(1) The Kingdom of God in the Synoptic teaching is present and future. Indissolubly linked with the Kingdom of God is the figure of the Son of Man, whose coming is also present and future. Through Him God's age-long purpose for mankind was unveiled and through Him it is to be accomplished. 'In the Gospel,' writes Marcion,[1] 'the Kingdom of God is Christ Himself', and Origen in his commentary on St Matthew[2] speaks of Jesus as '*autobasileia*'—the ideal of the Kingdom. This equation of Jesus and the Kingdom applies to the Kingdom as present and future. At every stage of fulfilment, Christ comes and gathers up in Himself the fruits of victory. The Kingdom has thus one focus in the Incarnate life of Christ, His death, His resurrection and the gift of the Spirit, and the other in the Parousia.

[1] Tertullian, *Adv. Marcion*, IV.33.
[2] *Matthew Tom.*, XIV.7; cf. *Theol. Wort.*, art. 'Basillia', p. 591.

(2) The Parousia, or the presence of Jesus at the end of the present order or age, means judgement. In our interpretation of the coming of Christ in judgement we need to beware of false analogies. The idea of an assize in which all generations are brought up for trial obviously cannot be envisaged on this earth. Further, while a trial is necessary for the operation of human justice, since the judge and jury need to gather information about the accused, no such process is conceivable where judgement is committed to God's Messiah. The verdict is known. It cannot be other than it is. The trial is now going on and the verdict accompanies the trial.[3] What we speak of as the last judgement implies that the verdict is made luminous by the relation in which we stand to the Son of Man.[4] The story of the separation of the sheep and the goats in Matthew $25^{31ff.}$ is not strictly speaking a picture of the Final Judgement, since the relative position of the sheep and the goats has already been determined before what is usually described as the 'trial' begins. What is distinctive in this passage is the underlying conviction that the trial has an end, and that the verdict is determined by the attitude of men to Christ in the ordinary relationships of human life—'Inasmuch as ye did it unto one of these my brethren, even these least, ye did it into me.' 'Inasmuch as ye did it not unto one of these least, ye did it not unto me.'

The 'Judgement' is universal and embraces previous generations as well as those who were personally encountered by the Son of Man in his earthly ministry. In the final scene, the Queen of the South and the men of Nineveh will be summoned, and their destiny will be determined by their attitude to the Eternal Rule of God in so far as it had been manifested in their day (Mt $12^{41f.}$=Lk $11^{31f.}$). The criterion in every generation is fidelity to the claims of the Kingdom of God, and since the Kingdom of God is Christ, all generations are under His judgement.

(3) The Parousia implies the final victory of goodness. There is no suggestion in the Synoptic teaching that, as the result of an evolutionary process, evil will be gradually eliminated and yield to the establishment of the Kingdom of God. Nor is there any

---

[3] cf. Quick, *Doctrines of the Creed* (1938), p. 253.

[4] The King (Mt $25^{34, 40}$) is the Son of Man (25^{31}) and the followers of Jesus are associated with him in the final scene (cf. Manson, *Teaching of Jesus*, p. 270).

justification for the view that there will be a final battle in which evil will be routed. Indeed, about the fate of Christian values in the present order there is no specific guidance given in the teaching of Jesus. The coming of the Son of Man will be sudden and unexpected. 'In an hour that ye think not, the Son of man cometh' (Lk 12^{40}, 17$^{23-30}$, 21$^{34-6}$). Arguments about the self-destructive character of evil have their place, but they are not the basis of the Christian hope as found in the teaching of Jesus. That hope is based upon the power, wisdom, and love of God, who is Sovereign Lord. The time and the fashion of the ultimate triumph of His Rule are known to Him alone.

It is inevitable that the question should be raised whether the final victory of goodness means that all men will be reconciled to the kingly Rule of God. In the gospels the evidence is conflicting, as indeed it is in the New Testament as a whole. The parables of the foolish virgins and of the wheat and the tares, the answer given to the question, 'Lord, are they few that be saved?' (Lk 13^{24}: 'For many, I say unto you, shall seek to enter in, and shall not be able'), and the story of the Rich Man and Lazarus, indicate a repudiation of universalism. On the other hand, we have the characteristic emphasis of Jesus upon the unrestricted love of God, illustrated by His teaching on forgiveness and by the parables of the lost sheep, the lost coin, and lost son. The shepherd goes after the sheep until he finds it, and the care of the shepherd for his sheep is but a pale reflexion of the unwearying persistence of divine love. We are not justified, however, in assuming that Jesus included in this and the other parables in Luke 15 a divine quest after death.

The references to future punishment in the Synoptic Gospels when taken as a whole are inconclusive, since they are relatively few and are couched in terms which admit of varying interpretations. Where the doctrine of everlasting punishment seems to be decisively taught, we can trace the influence of current Apocalyptic teaching. But the idea of reward in the future is represented in the Synoptic tradition, and the idea of reward has as its correlative the idea of punishment. The teaching of Jesus certainly leaves us in no manner of doubt about the devastating consequences of sin and of its ultimate frustration.

There are certain passages in the teaching of Jesus which might be taken as not excluding the idea of annihilation and 'conditional immortality'. The passage about blasphemy against the Holy Ghost (Mk 3^{28}; Mt 12^{31}, Lk 12^{10}) admits of such an interpretation. The supreme tragedy of sin that is left unchecked is the destruction of moral insight, and it is vain to offer forgiveness to anyone who has deprived himself of the capacity to discern its meaning. It must, however, be said, that the doctrine of conditional immortality is difficult to harmonize with the Christian revelation of God as Sovereign Love. First, it tends to obscure the fact that eternal life is the gift of God and not the reward of merit. Secondly, the force of the conviction that God is to be all in all is neutralized if victory is to be gained by the extinction of the recalcitrant.

Nevertheless, we cannot affirm that all will respond to the grace of God, although, in the interval between the Incarnation and the final coming of the Son of Man in glory, the Church is called to a world mission—'The Gospel must first be preached unto all the nations' (Mk 13^{10}). The result of the mission lies outside the boundaries of our knowledge, and prophecy is vain. No response to the Gospel of the Kingdom can be contemplated other than that which is freely given. The Son of Man, at every stage of His journey to the end toward which history moves, works by love and love alone, and there is no compulsion in love. If love were to seek to compel by methods other than those which involve a direct personal appeal to the mind and conscience, it would cease to be itself and would suffer ignominious defeat. The only victory which the enemies of our Lord could have achieved would have been to bring Him down to their level so that He used the weapons of their warfare and not His own. Because God is love, and because man while he remains man has the power to decline His call, we cannot say that all will be reconciled to His will. The belief that 'all will be saved' may be entertained as a hope but not as a dogma. Here we are in the realm of hidden things, and our faith is better exemplified by reverent agnosticism than by the dogmatic pronouncements which the Church is too often cajoled into making. The mode or time of God's final victory over evil in all its forms no man knoweth. But our confidence that victory is assured is based upon what He has already accomplished in the death and resurrection of Christ. The foundation of our faith in the Parousia lies in the triumph of Jesus over sin and death.

(4) The Parousia marks the end of the present order. Our Lord, as we saw, took over from Apocalyptic the conception of the two æons or ages—the present age and the age to come. If instead of associating the Parousia with the end of the world, which is taken to mean the end of history and the destruction of the physical universe, we were to connect it with the end of the present era or order, we should be nearer the thought of the New Testament. The present age or æon is a period of time, but it is primarily the expression of a purpose or way of life which is opposed to the will of God. Evil powers have infected man and nature, and the baneful results of their ascendancy are everywhere to be seen. The present order or dispensation is, and must be, under the judgement of God, and its affairs are to be brought to a conclusion which is in harmony with the righteous will of God. Further, the scene of the divine victory which brings the present age to a close is the earth, where Christ lived and died, and where He rose again. Nevertheless the end of the present order does not mean the end of history, unless history is to be unjustifiably identified with the present order. If history is the sphere in which the divine purpose for mankind is realized, the end of the present order means, not the end of history, but the inauguration of a new order or dispensation.

(5) The Parousia gives place to the final establishment of the Kingdom of God. Of the nature and conditions of life in the new age the Gospels tell us little that is specific and explicit. We are not left, however, without some knowledge of the quality of life shared by those who have entered into the Kingdom of God. There is but one Kingdom, whether it be regarded as present or future, and its character was manifested in Christ. The end or goal of the whole process of history has been revealed in Him, and those who are now living under the Rule of God which is a present reality have begun to taste the powers of the age to come. In the light of the revelation of the Rule of God in Christ and of the experience of the Church as the community of the Kingdom, we may seek to describe the nature of life in the era which marks the consummation of God's Kingly Rule.

(i) Life in the Kingdom of God is the gift of God. It cannot be claimed or earned. It is a gift to be received in humility and gratitude—'Except ye turn, and become as little children, ye shall in no wise enter into the kingdom of heaven' (Mt 18³). If the teaching of Jesus can be interpreted as implying universal survival, it has nothing to do with the belief that man by nature inherits eternal life. The doctrine of the natural immortality of the soul, when advanced by Christian thinkers, is the outcome, not of reflection upon the Christian revelation of God, but upon the nature of the soul considered apart from that revelation. Eternal life, or life in a divine dimension, in this world and in the world to come is dependent on the grace of God. We are not born by nature into this life, but raised to it by the power of God. What Christianity offers is not the promise of immortality through the possession by man of some element within his constitution which is imperishable, but the assurance of being raised together with Christ through the complete submission of mind and body to God's kingly Rule. The Christian doctrine of the future life is a doctrine of resurrection, and resurrection is the free gift of God.

(ii) Life in the Kingdom of God means communion with God through Jesus Christ. First, this implies the preservation of individuality, since communion involves a personal relationship between God and man. God is the God of Abraham, Isaac, and Jacob (Mk 12²⁶), and His ultimate purpose for man finds its fulfilment in a fellowship in which individuality is not destroyed but enhanced. There is a tradition in Christian and Eastern mysticism which looks to the breaking-down of all barriers between God and man as the consummation of human blessedness. This goal cannot claim biblical authority. In the Old Testament and the New, there is a gulf fixed between the human and the divine. The conception of a covenant presupposes the idea of difference as well as that of kinship. Indeed, absorption excludes communion, since it means the extinction of human personality with its distinctive qualities and relative independence. Where man is merged in God, he loses the capacity to experience the blessedness of union with God which is held to be his final goal. Secondly, communion with God is mediated by Jesus Christ at every stage of our spiritual progress in the Kingdom of God. Through union with Him in whom the age-long purpose for man was fulfilled, we are brought to God and enabled to live in obedience to His Rule. As we dwell in Him and as He dwells in us, we share the fruits of His perfect communion with God, and as through His mediation we begin our life in the Kingdom, so through becoming united to Him we grow in the knowledge of God and share the divine life. To be in fellowship with Christ is to have immediate communion with God in His kingly Rule, since the Kingdom of God is Christ.

Thirdly, although here and now we have an earnest or instalment of life in the Kingdom, the distinction between this life and life in the age to come should not be blurred. In the present order, the Christian is beset by temptation and conflict. He is conscious of the challenge of a world that is organized apart from God. He recalls that Jesus Himself was perplexed as He strove to discover the divine will, and that those who live near to God confess that clouds and darkness are round about His throne. This earthly order veils the truth about God and ourselves. The final coming of the Kingdom of God is marked by the victory of perfect love, which creates an order in which we may see God, not as in a glass darkly, but face to face.

(iii) Life in the Kingdom of God is corporate. Communion with God, which is the supreme gift of the Kingdom, implies the communion of saints. To be in fellowship with God is to be in a personal relationship of love with the children of His household which is the Church, here and in the life to come. The fellowship of the Church on earth is marred by divisions, some of which are due to sin, some to ignorance, and some perhaps to circumstances past and present beyond our control. And yet there are occasions, rare though they may be, when we gain a glimpse of what fellowship may mean when our union with God in Christ is complete. It may be a meeting for prayer in which those present are oblivious of themselves and desire only to wait upon God and learn His will. They become united to one another by bonds which cannot be broken and have a foretaste of the fellowship that is to be. Or, it may be a communion service at some international conference in which men and women of different races and of varying social and cultural status gather at the table of the Lord. The life of the age to come breaks into the present world. The veil is torn aside, and we are granted a vision of fellowship in worship, centred in the Cross, among the redeemed in heaven.

The fellowship of Christians on earth is inevitably restricted in scope by the conditions of human existence. While we need to be increasingly impatient of needless divisions and to explore every avenue that leads to the unity of the Church of Christ, we also have to reckon with the fact that fellowship with Christians separated by vast distances as well as by the strain of varying traditions cannot reach its consummation in the world as at present constituted. Even in a relatively small community, if our fellowship is to touch the depths, it is necessary to limit its range. We are all familiar with the type of person described by the late Dr. Inge as an honorary member of every religion and a humble adherent of none. Those who try to know everybody in the town in which they live hardly know anybody. Knowledge takes time. It involves concentration, and concentration means a measure of exclusion. We have also to bear in mind that the fellowship we enjoy here is only a small part of the wider fellowship of the Church on earth and in heaven. Communion with the saints in heaven is an integral element in Christian life and worship, but it is not of the same order as our communion with each other. Even if the claim could be established that in our communion with the Church in heaven we are able to identify those whom we may name, the number is relatively small. In the Church on earth, we glimpse, but only glimpse, the fellowship of the new age, which is free from the limitations of the present phase of historic existence.

Further, the fulfilment of Christian fellowship is dependent, not only upon the removal of earthly limitations, but upon the completion of the society of the redeemed. In later Jewish thought, represented in the literature between the Testaments, the Jews looked to the climax of history in the establishment of God's order of righteousness. That new order, they came to see, would not be an earthly Utopia enjoyed by those who happened to be alive on Doomsday. The righteous dead would share its blessings. There were various views as to the intermediate address of the previous generations of the righteous, but what signified was that it was believed that they would be raised to take their place in the Kingdom to be inaugurated by God. This conception of the relation of the individual to the society of the faithful, shorn of its accretions, was woven into the Christian picture of the age to come. While the Christian enters into the Kingdom at the moment he responds to the call of God in Christ, the fellowship of the life of heaven cannot be consummated until the society of the Kingdom is complete. When all are 'in Christ' and under

His Rule, the breadth and length and height and depth of God's sovereign love, and the full splendour and range of Christian fellowship, will be unveiled.

Corporateness is a distinctive feature of the Christian hope and is plainly set forth in the teaching of Jesus. The Kingdom of God implies a society, and everything which He taught about the Rule of God suggests that He envisaged a society in which the common relationship of men to God would be reflected and validated in their personal relationships. In the scant references among the words of Jesus to the conditions of life after the Parousia and the Judgement, the analogy of a feast, often a wedding feast, is used.[5] The patriarchs and prophets of every generation, with men from the four quarters of the earth, will sit down in the Kingdom of God and share its light and joy. In the eschatological saying attached to the Marcan account of the Last Supper (14^{25})—'I will no more drink of the fruit of the vine, until that day when I drink it new in the kingdom of God'—Jesus looks to the perfect fellowship which will be found when the Kingdom of God is consummated.

The corporate element in the Christian hope, which is central in the teaching of the New Testament, soon suffered eclipse, although it was still retained as part of the Christian creed and represented in the liturgies of the Church. Interest was transferred to the fate of the individual after death, and the vision of a transfigured universe which would be the scene of a fellowship reflecting the eternal purpose of God was sadly obscured. Though there was some understanding of the solidarity of evil, there seemed to be little appreciation of the solidarity of those who are, in Christ, destined to find their fulfilment at the final coming of the Kingdom of God. Preoccupation with the moment of death as it affected the future of the individual induced a blindness to the activity of God in history, and to the cosmic as well as the social aspects of redemption. Eschatology was thus concerned, not with the restitution of all things, but with an individualistic concern about death, judgement, heaven and hell, and it is not surprising that the rediscovery of the doctrine of the Church and of cosmic eschatology has followed upon a revival of biblical theology. We shall not, however, succeed in safeguarding the

---

[5] Lk 13^{29}=Mt 8^{11}; Mt 22^{1-14}; Lk 14^{16-24}; cf. for the metaphor of the feast: *Eth. En.* 62^{14}, *2 Baruch* $29^{5ff.}$; *2 Esdras* $6^{51ff.}$; *Pirke Aboth*, 3^{20}.

Christian hope against false interpretation by denigrating the individual, or by minimizing the crucial significance of the encounter of the individual soul with God. God confronts the individual in Christ and demands a decision. That is the moment that decides our destiny. If we answer the call, we are brought within the fellowship of His Kingdom, which is the Church, and we become associated with Christ and all who are His brethren in His advancing reign, 'till we all attain unto the unity of the faith, and of the knowledge of the Son of God, unto a fullgrown man, unto the measure of the stature of the fulness of Christ' (Eph 4^{13}). That is the perfection of fellowship in the Kingdom of God.

(iv) Life in the Kingdom of God means fulfilment. The Christian hope implies the continuation, not the end, of history, and the activity of God in the whole course of human history will be gathered into the life of the Kingdom when it is consummated. 'I came,' said Jesus, 'not to destroy, but to fulfil' (Mt 5^{17}), and these words may be applied to His coming in glory. The 'present age', which in the New Testament extends from the Fall to the Parousia, is under condemnation, and Jesus and his disciples believed that they were living in the last days. But we are not to suppose that the end of the present age means nothing but judgement. Everything that God has wrought within that age in the material universe and in the life of man will be carried to fulfilment in a reconstituted universe, a new heaven and a new earth. The figure of a banquet used by our Lord to describe life in the Kingdom suggests the joy and satisfaction of an age of fulfilment, which brings with it new opportunities and provides a stage which is adequate for the ends of Sovereign Love (Lk 19^{12-27}).

Fulfilment does not exclude growth and creative activity. The question is often raised as to whether the life to come as conceived by Christianity is a life of rest or conflict, of quest or achievement. No doubt the Christian tradition as embodied in hymns and theological writings seems to imply that rest will be the main feature of heaven, and while the prospect of unending relaxation or peaceful contemplation undisturbed by frustrated aims appeals to some, it depresses others. The oft-quoted words of R. L. Stevenson in *Virginibus Puerisque*—To travel hopefully is a better thing than to arrive, and the true success is to labour—express a sentiment that is widely shared. What, it may be asked, will there be left to live for unless there is something to fight against? When there are no obstacles to stir us to action, no trials to test our endurance, no victories to be won, will not life become static and insipid? We tend to overlook the fact that spiritual progress does not cease when there is no longer an enemy within or without to be vanquished. Life in the Kingdom of God is life in communion with God who is Sovereign Love, and it provides abundant opportunity for exploration and discovery. The love of God is not exhausted even by the Incarnation, and in the Kingdom of God its nature will be progressively revealed. At every stage we may expect some new manifestation of God's purpose, which will awaken gratitude and praise, enrich our understanding, and quicken our aspiration. Love is ever creative, and when the final victory over the powers of evil has taken place, the energies of love, unchanging yet ever new, will be set free to act on their own scale.

The age-long purpose of God cannot be fulfilled other than through history, and its consummation takes place in this world transfigured in all its relations by the power of God. Although the fashion of this world passes away, the world is not to be destroyed but transformed. This conception of the universe and its future is based upon the New Testament writings, and implied in the teaching of Jesus and in the doctrine of the Incarnation. No doubt the cosmology of the New Testament is at variance with our modern ideas of the universe, but its eschatology was grounded in the revelation of God's power and glory in the death and resurrection of Christ. When the Christian hope as there set forth has been unclothed or demythologized, there remains the conviction that the divine purpose is the re-creation and renewal of the whole body and texture of the universe, so that the cosmic order may be restored to its true centre as the sphere of life in the Kingdom of God.

The final coming of the Kingdom means the dawn of a new era of history, and it is here that we are confronted by the relation of the transfigured universe of Christian hope to space and time. History involves a time-process, and since for many the life to come is associated with timeless existence, it is assumed that the consummated Kingdom means the end of history. First, it is to be observed that eternity in the sense of timeless existence cannot be the medium of the revelation of the purpose of the living God for mankind. The goal of history is dynamic and not static, and is revealed through history which involves the time-process. God Himself transcends space and time, but the relations of space and time are not to be regarded as alien or even as accidental to the divine Rule, since within the framework which they provide, God has disclosed His purpose to mankind. Secondly, although we may infer that there are fundamental differences between the conditions of life in the two 'ages' (Mk 12^{25}), we are not justified in assuming that in the age to come time yields to timelessness, or even that spatial relations are done away. If, in the Kingdom of God, individuality is to be preserved and there is to be growth in the knowledge of God and in our communion with one another, it is difficult to grasp how the idea of time can be eliminated.

Time in the Kingdom of God, here or beyond, is not a matter of chronology or successive instants registered by the clock or almanac. It is a question of moments charged with divine significance. The Christian hope contains the promise of the fulfilment of time and its redemption from a meaningless successiveness. In the lives of the saints we have abundant evidence of what we may describe as the sacramental use of time. Every moment becomes an opportunity for a meeting with God and is thus woven into the texture of His unchanging purpose. Baron von Hügel, in stressing the need for finding in the passing moment a gift of God, recalls how Goethe's mother, Frau Rath, when a friend ignorant of her condition called at the door and asked to see her, sent down the message: Frau Rath is busy dying. 'Indeed,' adds von Hügel, 'a genial quiet death to self lies in every minute, when the minute is thus taken separately as the dear will and the direct vehicle of God.' Frau Rath knew the difference between '*chronos*' and '*kairos*', and had already a foretaste of the experience of time in the age to come.[6]

Again, if we cannot exclude in our thought of life in the Kingdom the idea of time, it is only a little less difficult to eliminate the concept of space. Our individuality in present experience

---

[6] cf. von Hügel, *Essays and Addresses* (1926), II.227; and R. N. Flew, *The Idea of Perfection*, for an excellent treatment of the principle of concentration on each moment (pp. 405ff.).

is associated with our bodies which are localized in space, and fellowship is a relationship between individuals who function from different centres in space. It may be said at once that this suggests the belief in the resurrection of the body. If by the re-resurrection of the body is meant the resuscitation of the elements which compose our earthly bodies, the implication is obviously to be denied. But if by the body is meant a medium which can be identified and which conditions our individuality and our communion with one another, far from denying the implication, we would affirm it.

The early Christians, in whose life the hope of the restoration of all things was a dominant feature, were not concerned with the difficult philosophical and scientific questions which confront us today in our attempt to interpret the meaning of the consummation of the Kingdom of God. Their conviction that all things had been made through Christ and unto Him, was born, not of speculation or a dispassionate review of the course of history, but of the assurance that in the mighty acts of God wrought in Christ the new era had already dawned, and that they were living within it. History was not to be discarded, since its meaning had now been disclosed and the future age would unveil its true and full significance. They were themselves witnesses of the forces of renewal already in operation in the life of the Church. They were children of the Resurrection, and it was their faith that He who had raised Jesus from the dead would bring all things into subjection to His will. By that faith they lived and in that faith they died.

In our own day, the Christian hope is being challenged by secular philosophies of hope which exercise a widespread influence in every land. There are those who look for salvation in the dissociation of the ideals of justice, truth, equality and freedom from their theological context in the Christian Faith, and who believe that in the pursuit of these ideals, unhampered by the incubus of dogma and aided by the resources released by modern science, we shall find the secret of world peace and happiness. With this view the Church has some measure of sympathy, and it is important that every inch of common ground should be explored by Christians and non-Christians. It must be regretfully admitted that the Church, although it is committed to the values which are enshrined in the philosophy of humanism in its nobler forms, has too often been fitful in its witness to their reality, and has been more concerned to secure a correct formulation of its faith and order than to relate its message to the life of the world. If there is today a conflict between science and religion, a major part of the responsibility rests with the Church, which, in the not very distant past, either by-passed science as irrelevant to social redemption, or declared war upon the scientific attitude as such. And yet it must be recognized that a humanistic philosophy based on the values which have been built up into the life of Western culture is a philosophy of despair and not of hope. As soon as the question of the ultimate authority of these ideals is raised—and it is being raised on all sides today—humanism has no satisfying answer. Unless this world is the expression of a purpose which has its roots in that which is unchanging, men will not indefinitely regard justice and right and truth as sacred. These values suffer deterioration and change their meaning when they are dissociated from religious faith. Justice comes to mean insisting upon our rights, equality a way of thinking that other people are no better than we are, and truth a relative standard that can be manipulated in our own interests. Secular humanism in its various forms ignores the realities of a human situation that is vitiated by self-interest as well as by ignorance, and within that situation there is no power which can change the direction of the lives of men.

Communism, which is proclaimed in many lands as the gospel of hope, is persuaded that there is no salvation in the present order. There is only one remedy for an order based on capitalist interests and that is to bring it to a speedy close, even though its death may be preceded by conflict and suffering which only an Apocalyptist writer could fittingly describe. The Communist faith affirms the reality of the material world and teaches that history has a purpose which can be discerned; it is universal in its scope and looks to the consummation of heroic sacrifice in the birth of a new order. Some of the characteristics of Communist philosophy have encouraged the misleading notion that Communism is a Christian heresy. The Christian heresies have as a rule been confined to differing interpretations of particular Christian doctrines, and some heretics have believed that they were defending the faith once delivered more faithfully than their orthodox opponents. Communism as a total philosophy repudiates every article of the Creed, and we obscure the issue if we speak of such a world-view as a Christian heresy.

Christianity differs from Communism in its conception of the goal of history and the way to its attainment. Like Communism, it affirms, as we have seen, the reality of material needs, and if the Church had kept in full view the nature of the Christian hope as an order in which all things, spiritual and material, are to be gathered up into the divine purpose, Communism would not today be occupying ground that was too easily abandoned by those who professed allegiance to the Incarnate Lord. Man must eat to live. But is that the last word about man? If it is, then in spite of his superior intelligence, he is reduced to the animal level. And if bread is made an end in itself, and if the quest for it is taken out of the wider context of the Kingdom of God where it is set in the Lord's Prayer, it will become the symbol and source of strife, war, and the power which invariably corrupts. Again, like Communism, Christianity holds no brief for the present order and looks beyond it for redemption. Here, however, we encounter a fundamental difference. While Christianity looks for the redemption of society to a power that is not of this world, Communism still expects salvation from this world alone and imagines that human nature in its unregenerate state can be its vehicle. The 'glory yet to come' of Communism, for which past generations are sacrificed and scrapped so that only those who survive the woes that precede the messianic age will enjoy its fruits, stands in marked contrast to the age of glory of the Christian hope, in which freedom and order are reconciled, and each man in union with Christ and with Christians of all ages finds himself and his brethren in the joyous and creative life of complete devotion to the Rule of God.

It would be foolish to underestimate the strength of the forces ranged against the Kingdom of God in the present age, even though the eye of faith perceives Christ reigning as King and recalls His word before the high priest: 'You shall see the Son of Man seated at the right hand of power and coming with the clouds of heaven.' The ultimate issue is not in doubt for those to whom Christ has already come in His redeeming power. The Church, however, can take but little comfort from this assurance, unless the powers of the age to come are manifest in its daily life and witness, and unless it is striving to set forth with insight and heroic enterprise the unchanging Gospel in worship and prayer, in fellowship and social witness, and indeed in all human relations. Although we need not wait for the coming of a reunited Church before we address ourselves to the World Mission of the Church, nothing short of a Church that is visibly one, holy, catholic and apostolic, can accomplish the task which the Lord of the new age has entrusted to us. To this generation has been granted a rich and spacious conception of the Kingdom of God which links us afresh to the Church of the New Testament. Dare we limit ourselves to a fragment of the vision which we have received, or ask for a more convenient commission? If we decline the divine call which comes through the rediscovery of the Word of God in the Scriptures and the pressure of world events, Christianity may be submerged for an indefinite period. A civilization dies, it has been said, when men do not anticipate the possibility of its death, and that is true of a Christian civilization. There is still time; for the end is not yet. The Church cannot save the world, but given a Church that is completely committed to its vocation as the organ of the Kingdom of God, there is no limit to what God is able to accomplish through its witness.

INDICES

INDEX OF NAMES

Barth, K., 73
Baillie, D. M., 80, 82
Barrett, C. K., 86n., 87
Bruce, A. B., 11
Brunner, E., 69, 89–91
Bultmann, R., 74, 75

Cadoux, C. J., 97n.
Charles, R. H., 14
Clogg, F. B., 26n.
Cullmann, O., 73, 94

Dalman, G., 17
Dobschütz, E. von, 16
Dodd, C. H., 18, 19, 29, 74
Dougall, L., 16

Emmett, C., 16

Farmer, H. H., 51
Flemington, W. F., 58n.
Flew, R. N., 28n., 39, 40, 86n., 87–8, 94n., 114

George, A. R., 36n.
Glasson, T. F., 35n.
Gloege, G., 17
Glover, T. R., 16

Harnack, A., 12, 13, 72
Hermann, W., 10
Higgins, A. J. B., 65n.
Hoyle, F., 46
Hügel, F. von, 48, 114

Jeremias, J., 97

Kaftan, J., 10, 72
Kittel, G., 17n.
Kohn, K. G., 24

Manson, T. W., 32, 36, 92–3, 96n., 104

Marcion, 103
Matthews, W. R., 77ff.
Milligan, G., 102
Moffatt, J., 15
Moulton, J. H., 102
Munck, J., 97n.

Nygren A., 49–50

Otto, R., 17, 29, 40

Pusey, E. B., 50

Quick, O. C., 104

Relton, H. M., 69
Renan, J. E., 11
Ritschl, A., 9, 70, 71

Sanday, W., 15
Schmidt, K. L., 17
Scott, C. A., 26n., 37
Scott, E. F., 15, 87
Schweitzer, A., 9, 13–15, 16
Seeley, J. R., 10
Smith, W. R., 40
Snaith, N. H., 49n.
Stout, G. F., 52
Strauss, D. F., 11, 12
Streeter, B. H., 15, 16
Swete, H. B., 15

Taylor, V., 25, 64, 86n., 87, 98
Temple, W., 37
Tertullian, 103
Thomasius, G., 72
Tillich, P., 74–5

Weiss, J., 9, 12
Wellhausen, J., 16

INDEX OF SCRIPTURE REFERENCES

(a) OLD TESTAMENT

Exodus
3^{14}...24
24^8...63

1 Chronicles
29^{11}...21

Psalms
2^7...42
22^{28}...21
42^7...58

103^{19}...21
110^1...34
145^{13}...21

Isaiah
42^1...42
43^2...58
55^9...26

Ezekiel
$31^{3,\,6,\,12}$...39
34^{12-24}...40

Jeremiah
31^{33}...41

Daniel
4^{12}...39
$7^{13\text{ff}}$...16, 31, 34
$7^{27\text{ff}}$...21

Micah
5^4...39

(b) NEW TESTAMENT

Matthew
3^{13-17}...42
5^{17}...112
5^{32}...28
5^{43-5}...26
$6^{12\text{ff}}$...37
7^{11}...86
8^{11}...35, 111
9^{1-6}...40
10^1...96
10^7...30
10^{20}...86
10^{33}...34
10^{35}...28
$10^{37\text{ff}}$...33
11^{2-11}...30
$11^{12\text{ff}}$...39
11^{27}...31
12^{28}...30, 86
12^{31}...86, 106
12^{32}...86
$12^{41\text{ff}}$...30, 104
13^{16}...30
13^{24-30}...39
13^{47-50}...39
$16^{17\text{ff}}$...93
18^3...108
18^5...96
18^{8-9}...28
18^{23-35}...37
20^{1-16}...26
21^{31}...39
22^{1-14}...111
23^{34-6}...33
23^{38}...33
$25^{31\text{ff}}$...34, 104
26^{29}...59
26^{38}...63

$26^{40\text{ff}}$...64
26^{60b-1}...40

Mark
1^{9-11}...42
1^{15}...30
3^{14-15}...92, 95, 96
3^{28}...106
3^{29}...86
4^{30-2}...39
6^{7-13}...40, 92
7^{9-13}...28
7^{18}...97
7^{21-3}...37
8^{31}...58, 59
8^{38}...34
9^{37}...96
9^{43-7}...28, 39
10^{2-12}...28
10^{15}...28
10^{29}...28
10^{33}...58
10^{37}...93
10^{38}...58
$10^{39\text{ff}}$...33
10^{42}...93
11^{25}...37
12^{1-9}...39
$12^{26\text{ff}}$...35
13^{10}...106
13^{11-13}...33, 86
14^{21}...59
14^{24}...63
14^{25}...35, 59, 65, 111
14^{34}...64
14^{36}...60

14^{38}...64
14^{41}...59
14^{58}...40
14^{62}...34, 60

Luke
3^{21-2}...42
6^{27-8}...26
6^{32-6}...26
7^{18-30}...30
7^{34}...32
7^{41-3}...37
9^{1-6}...40, 96
9^{10}...92
9^{48}...96
9^{58}...32
$10^{1\text{ff}}$...40, 94
10^{8-9}...30
$10^{23\text{ff}}$...30
11^{13}...86
11^{20}...30, 86
11^{31}...30, 104
11^{49-51}...33
12^9...34
12^{10}...86, 106
12^{12}...86
12^{32}...39
12^{40}...37
12^{50}...58
12^{53}...28
13^{29}...111
13^{35}...33
14^{16-24}...111
14^{26}...33
16^{16}...39
16^{18}...28

Luke
17^{22-30}...34, 105
18^{8b}...34
18^{9-14}...27
19^{12-27}...40
19^{41-4}...33

21^{15}...86
21^{34-6}...105
22^{18}...59, 65
$22^{29\text{ff}}$...65
$22^{45\text{f}}$...64

1 *Corinthians*
11^{25}...63
15^{25}...103

Ephesians
4^{13}...112

JEWISH WRITERS
1 Enoch 62^{14}...111
2 Baruch $29^{5\text{ff}}$...111
2 Esdras $6^{51\text{ff}}$...111
Pirke Aboth, 3^{20}...111

www.ingramcontent.com/pod-product-compliance
Lightning Source LLC
Chambersburg PA
CBHW072159160426
43197CB00012B/2445